Invite the Bully To Tea

End harassment, bullying and dysfunction forever
with a simple yet radical new approach

Maureen F. Fitzgerald, PhD

CP

CENTERPOINT MEDIA

2015

Praise for this book

"…an extremely useful book – a practical, step-by-step guide to facilitating conflict conversations that can be used by any manager, team or organization to turn conflicts into collaborations…
It is a "must-read" for anyone who wants to improve workplace communications."
Kenneth Cloke and Joan Goldsmith, authors of *Resolving Conflicts at Work: Eight Strategies for Everyone on the Job*

"Fitzgerald is at the cutting edge of bringing restorative practices to corporations. She provides wonderful real life examples as well as an overview of how-to do it."
Ted Wachtel, co-author of *Toughlove*, author of *Real Justice* and President of the International Institute for Restorative Practices

"Finally a book that reveals how circles are readily adaptable to the challenges corporations and government organizations encounter every day. Fitzgerald's book is a must not just for managers but for anyone seeking to build respectful, productive relationships within any work environment."
Barry Stuart, co-author of *Peacemaking Circles,* retired judge, CSE Consulting Group

"I believe that Circles can promote more complete and successful resolution of many organization conflicts by creating a safe space for people to "tell their stories.""
Gary Harper, author of *The Joy of Conflict Resolution*

"This practical resource [is a] simple, step-by-step approach to building workplace relationships, resolving conflict and improving morale. It's a most valuable read for today's managers, human resources personnel, in-house counsel and facilitators."
Sally Campbell, Mediator/Lawyer and Facilitator

CenterPoint Media
Vancouver, BC
Canada
www.CenterPointInc.com

LIBRARY AND ARCHIVES CANADA CATALOGUING IN PUBLICATION

Fitzgerald, Maureen F., author
    Invite the Bully to Tea: End harassment, bullying and dysfunction forever with a simple yet radical new approach/ Maureen F. Fitzgerald

Previously published under the title: Corporate circles.
Includes bibliographical references.
Issued in print and electronic formats.

ISBN   978-0-9939840-1-3 (paperback)
ISBN   978-1-988072-05-0 (e-book)

    1. Conflict management. 2. Harassment--Prevention.
3. Bullying in the workplace--Prevention. 4. Communication in organizations. 5. Teams in the workplace. I. Title.

HD42.F583 2015   658.3'145   C2015-905717-5   C2015-905718-3

Layout and design: Duncan Watts-Grant
Cover design: Christine Unterthiner, Pilot Brand
Cover image: iStockphoto
Author photo: www.photobinphotography.com
Editing and proofreading: Suzanne Doyle Ingram

Contents

This book is dedicated to the peacemakers of the world, and of course my life teacher Paul.

Out beyond the ideas of doing right doing and wrong doing, there is a field. I'll meet you there.

— Rumi

Peace cannot be kept by force. It can only be achieved by understanding.

— Albert Einstein

Preface

In this book I introduce a unique and powerful way of dealing with group conflict. Instead of running from conflict or trying to manage it, I ask you to sit with it and work through it together as a group. In essence I ask you to "invite the bully to tea" just as the Buddha did on the night before his enlightenment when rather than ignore or fight evil (Mara) as he had done in the past, calmly invited him for tea.

Several years ago I was practicing law and had established myself as an expert in bullying and harassment. I became very good at investigating workplaces, interviewing traumatized employees and writing detailed reports about what was happening in the workplace. The aim of most of these investigations (as directed by corporate policy) was to establish guilt and apply blame. If I found a person "guilty," this person was usually penalized or removed from the workplace. This is the adversarial model I had grown accustomed to as a lawyer.

After a few years, I began to realize that these investigations did not address many of the problems and were, in some situations, causing more problems. As I began to look for better ways to resolve these deep-rooted types of workplace conflict I came upon "conferencing." Conferencing is a criminal process in which accused offenders have a conversation with the people they have harmed. The offender and the victim then create a solution that works for both. As a result, both people are able to move forward.

I began applying this process in my work and the results were amazing. As I brought people together in what I called Corporate Circles, they challenged their assumptions about others, they discovered hidden perceptions about what was happening, and they talked about their shared values and particularly the importance of fairness. I began to see empathy emerge naturally in each of the participants. As each person began to truly understand the impact of their behavior on others, they saw things differently and began to treat others better.

Now I have come to see other conflict resolution techniques such as training, conflict coaching and mediation as only partially effective at resolving deep-seated conflict. They go only so far to improve relations and create respectful workplaces, and they often take years to be effective.

It seems so much easier (and more cost-effective) to simply create a place where people feel safe enough to express how they really feel, get past the hard feelings they have been harboring and make a fresh start. This is what Corporate Circles provide.

If you are looking for a long-term solution to conflict and are finding that traditional methods of resolving disputes are not working, this book is for you. If you think that your group is not communicating openly and could be working much better together, keep reading.

CHAPTER 1

What is a Corporate Circle?

There are no problems we cannot solve together, and very few we can solve by ourselves.

— Lyndon B. Johnson

One does not discover new lands without consenting to lose the sight of the shore for a very long time.

— Andre Gide

In the middle of difficulty lies opportunity.

— Albert Einstein

This book introduces a method for resolving workplace conflict quickly and easily. It shows you how to hold a Corporate Circle—an effective, efficient and long-lasting way to resolve any corporate conflict. You will learn a step-by-step, proven strategy for creating conversations that resolve conflict, enhance trust and lead to mutually acceptable action plans for any difficult situation. This strategy can be used by executives, human resources people and managers in almost any group situation.

Each year corporations spend billions of dollars to try to resolve workplace conflict, yet many workplaces still harbor deep cultures of mistrust, where disputes are daily fare. Conflict surfaces as endless gossip, disagreements, uneasiness and disrespectful behavior. Unresolved conflict slowly erodes productivity and creativity and causes headaches at all levels of an organization. Although conflict is normal and can be productive, most is destructive and can cause a ripple effect across an organization. This is because most people avoid confrontation and are afraid to say what they really think.

Unlike other conflict resolution methods, Corporate Circles get to the real root of the problem—quickly. Through a candid conversation, the hidden rivers of lava that spark many volcano-like disputes are uncovered. In just a matter of hours, even the most dysfunctional group will be able to share opinions and perspectives and move past negative feelings, so they can begin to move forward.

This chapter describes what Corporate Circles are and how Circles can help you. At the end of the chapter is a list of questions and answers about Corporate Circles.

What Is a Corporate Circle?

A Corporate Circle involves a group of people having a courageous yet compassionate conversation. Unlike other meetings, in a Circle participants feel safe enough to talk about what is really important. They are able to move past any bad feelings so the group can become truly productive. A group will usually hold a Circle for one of the following reasons:

- to deal with ongoing or repeated issues at work
- to resolve a dispute between two or more people
- to rebuild damaged workplace relations
- to create a more cohesive and effective team

During a Corporate Circle participants sit in a circle and discuss the problems that are occurring in the workplace and the difficulties they are having in relating with others. Each person is given an opportunity to speak openly and candidly. Participants share their perceptions, opinions and feelings. The group specifically discusses what has been happening, how best to repair any harm and how to prevent future conflict. Each issue is canvassed through open dialogue. The Circle ends with the group creating an action plan. Although a group can participate in more than one Corporate Circle, one is usually sufficient for groups of less than twenty people.

How Corporate Circles Can Help You

The process sounds simple enough, but it can have powerful results. Using Corporate Circles in your workplace will help your organization do the following:

- transform conflict

- create trust and heal damaged relations

- build strong teams

- empower individuals and enhance personal accountability

- facilitate creative problem solving

Here are some of the reasons why and ways in which this happens.

Circles transform conflict

Circles are effective at transforming and not just resolving conflict for all of the following reasons.

- ***All those impacted by a particular conflict diagnose and resolve the problem.*** Conflict is rarely just a dispute between two people. Indeed, most workplace conflict is supported either directly or indirectly by many people. The most common support is through silence, or simply not acknowledging that there is a conflict.

Therefore conflict can only be resolved effectively by the participation of everyone involved in or impacted by it. This is the reason why so many two-person mediations fail. Even if these two people settle their differences, remnants of the conflict often linger that can be a catalyst for future conflict.

○ *Hidden causes of conflict are disclosed.* Conflict is rarely what it appears to be. What you see on the surface usually does not reflect the deeper causes of conflict. These causes often emerge over a period of time and are completely unique to the individuals involved and the particular context. No two conflicts are identical. In a Corporate Circle, perceptions are uncovered and hidden issues are raised and resolved. This happens as the group begins to formulate a *shared understanding* about what is happening, how people are impacted, and why they respond in certain ways.

○ *Emotions can be expressed safely.* Many people are afraid of emotions and do not know how to deal with them personally or in others. Thus they try to hide their feelings. This squelching of emotions causes people to bottle up their feelings and although it may seem useful in the short term, this has the potential for exacerbating to situation. Often these feeling linger and impact behaviors long after an event. Most organizations do not support or encourage the open expression of emotions. We are all expected to be extraordinarily rational and objective. We are expected to check our emotions at the door, regardless of our so-called personal situation. Corporate Circles work because they pay attention to the emotional and psychological aspects of conflict. A key component of a Circle is to allow participants to express their true feelings, especially when negative. The process almost always results in an apology or two and recognition by everyone in attendance that people have feelings. In essence, it allows people to vent.

○ *Participants learn how to resolve future conflict.* Because Circles allow whole groups to work together to resolve conflict, each person learns how their behavior impacts others so that future conflict is prevented or resolved without outside help. In other words, Circles empower employees to resolve future conflict. In addition, during a Circle each person learns many interpersonal skills. This happens by watching the facilitator and by actively participating in the dialogue. Each person has the opportunity to immediately practice the skills they are learning. These skills include empathetic listening, using the body to communicate understanding, staying silent, paraphrasing and mirroring, among others.

Circles create trust and heal damaged relations

Many workplaces harbor deep cultures of mistrust. Without trust, workplaces become fragmented institutions where individuals are only interested in protecting themselves and their jobs. This lack of trust destroys cooperation, negates the possibility of teamwork, and ultimately interferes with the effective operation of any organization. Ann Coombs in her book *The Living Workplace* suggests that this mistrust causes lethargy, absenteeism, and a fear-based workplace. She believes that erecting a barrier between feelings and "real life" causes many of the problems and "[r]efusing to admit natural human feelings, and tolerating the negative on the grounds that it is the only way to survive, deadens the human spirit."

The lack of trust comes from a loss of confidence in others or in the organization as a whole. It usually results from a number of situations that happen over an extended period of time. Sometimes the dissolution of trust is so slow and subtle that suddenly people wake up and realize they don't trust anyone around them.

The only way to rebuild trust is to reestablish connections between co-workers and engage as an organization? in activities that will demonstrate trustworthiness. Although this can take months and sometimes years, a Corporate Circle can speed up this process enormously.

The following analogy demonstrates the similarity between personal relationships and organizational relations in nurturing relations to build trust.

> **The piggy bank model.** Most relationships are like piggy banks. Each person in a relationship can make deposits or withdrawals from the relationship. Deposits are the activities that enhance a relationship. Withdrawals are activities that take away from a relationship. Like piggy banks, relationships can

range from being full to being completely empty. If a relationship is full, it is resilient and can withstand a good number of withdrawals before it will begin to fail. If the relationship is empty, one or both people must make deposits to keep it nourished. Dysfunctional relationships are like empty banks. If neither person is able or interested in making a contribution, the relationship will remain cold and distant. Ideally you want to keep a high level of deposits in those relationships you value. Indeed, you probably do this naturally. If you want to reestablish an injured relationship, you must start by making a deposit, no matter how small.

In order to reestablish relationships and build trust you must do three things. You must communicate in some way with the other person, you must get over any hard feelings, and you must engage in activities that will rebuild the trust you have lost. All three things happen in a Corporate Circle.

The first step—opening up communication—is often the most difficult, and Corporate Circles provide a place where this communication can happen. Circles also allow for the processing of any bad feelings. In Corporate Circles individuals talk about the impact of events and actions on themselves and others. They stop blaming and develop a sense of empathy that enables them to appreciate how other people think and feel. As they become more open to other perspectives, they feel more comfortable describing their own. This level of comfort and safety builds momentum toward a new common understanding.

This common understanding is the necessary foundation to building trusting relations.

The learning that occurs in the Circle extends well beyond the immediate discussion and often has a long-term impact. People tend to treat their colleagues better and in some situations begin to treat their families and neighbors better as well. Like the ripple effect of conflict there is a positive ripple effect.

Circles build strong teams

When people begin speaking to each other a number of things happen. First, people recognize others as fallible human beings—with needs and wants. Even individuals who do not like each other tend to relate on a fundamental level when they begin to converse. Second, by sharing information about themselves, they become more attractive and as a result others grow more curious. This curiosity and resulting understanding are the very things that build relationships and ultimately a sense of belonging. Without conversations, relationships are pretty much impossible.

As we learn about others we also begin to see a bigger picture and how we are connected at some level. This prompts a sense of caring and the entire relationship shifts. The relationship not only becomes more productive and easier but also more enjoyable.

Circles empower individuals and enhance accountability

The modern corporate structure is one of partnership rather

than hierarchy. The older models of command and control are being replaced by systems that empower individuals and teams. Author David Gergen calls the new approach "the influence model of leadership. Instead of picturing a leader at the top of pyramid, we envision her in the middle of a circle with spokes extending outward. Instead of hurling thunderbolts from atop Mount Olympus, the new leader persuades, empowers, collaborates and partners."

In this system every individual must become more responsible and accountable than ever before. Each must have a better understanding of their role in the group and their contribution to the organization.

This understanding is enhanced through a Corporate Circle. During these conversations, people sit in a circle where there is no top or bottom. Each person faces each other person and engages fully in a conversation with everyone else. They talk about what they do and how it relates to others in the Circle. Each person notices who is speaking and who is not. This causes shy people to step out and causes overbearing people to step back. It causes each person to be more accountable for their actions both in the Circle and outside the Circle.

There is no place in the Circle to be condescending or arrogant. The energy of a circle is by nature equal, and there is a natural tendency in a Circle to move toward harmony and balance. If one person tries to take control, the Circle responds in intriguing ways to neutralize that force.

Real life. Several years ago I was asked to facilitate two Circles – one to transform a long-term conflict among nine employees and the other to help the group design a strategy for moving forward. The first Circle went very well and everyone participated actively. The group compiled a list of ideas to be discussed in the next Circle. In the second Circle the manager, who was somewhat out spoken, spent most of the first hour explaining the problems with each of the proposed ideas. Finally one junior employee spoke up and shifted the entire conversation, prompting all of the others to join in. She said, "Jim you have been talking about the negatives for some time. It seems to me that whenever we suggest something you tell us why it will not work. Is it possible to just listen and keep an open mind to what we have to say?"

Circles facilitate creative problem solving

Because Corporate Circles provide a safe place for a conversation, creativity is permitted to surface and usually does. Through the course of the conversation people let go of their inhibitions—of saying something silly or offending others—and are more willing to canvass solutions that might not be articulated in a less safe place.

Near the end of a Corporate Circle, participants are asked to make suggestions about how to move forward. The ideas that pour out are amazing. This is partially because the group has engaged in a candid conversation and has developed a sense of security that supports risk taking.

This creative problem solving, like the improved employee

relations, also has a lasting impact. By simply engaging in the process of a Corporate Circle, much like team-building exercises, people are more inclined *outside* the Circle to voice creative ideas. In essence, the group learns how to take risks.

By being part of a Circle, each person leaves with not only an experience of a powerful conversation but also a confidence that these types of conversations can happen and are productive. Therefore, those who have been involved in a Circle will often suggest other ways to come together in conversation long after the Circle has passed. In other words, Circles foster more dialogue.

Corporate Circles at a Glance

Here are some frequently asked questions and answers about Corporate Circles.

What is a Corporate Circle?
A Corporate Circle is a meeting of a group of people who wish to resolve work-related issues or enhance working relations.

How does a Corporate Circle work?
During the Corporate Circle individuals share their thoughts, opinions and perceptions about what works, what does not work and how to make improvements. During a Circle many perceptions, which could be causing disagreements, are brought to light.

What is the process?

A facilitator is selected to manage the Corporate Circle process. The facilitator interviews those who are involved and selects those who will be in the Circle. A meeting date is set, the Circle is held, and the facilitator follows up afterwards. In some cases more than one Corporate Circle is necessary.

What happens at a Corporate Circle?

At a Corporate Circle the group sits in a circle and discusses what is happening in the workplace and any current conflicts. Each person is given an opportunity to speak openly and candidly. Each is invited to describe what has been happening, its impact on them and what they would like to see happen in the future.

What types of situations are most appropriate?

Work situations that benefit most from a Corporate Circle are those where conflict keeps arising, where old issues have not been resolved, where decision making seems impossible, or where recent events have damaged relationships.

Who should attend the Corporate Circle?

Any person who contributes to the effective working of the group or who is impacted by a situation or conflict should attend. This can include employees, managers, executives, CEOs and other stakeholders.

How long does a Corporate Circle last?

The length of a Corporate Circle depends on the nature of the situation and the number of participants. The facilitator will be able to assess the time needed after some initial interviews. A Circle usually lasts several hours.

What is the role of the facilitator?

The facilitator's role is to help the group discuss issues and consider solutions while keeping the conversation on track. At the end of the Circle the facilitator will help the group work out the details of how things can be improved, usually in the form of an agreement.

What are the results of a Corporate Circle?

A successful Corporate Circle can have the following results:

- transform conflict

- create trust and heal damaged work relations

- build strong teams

- empower individuals and enhance personal accountability

- facilitate creative problem solving skills

The next chapters discuss how to create, prepare for and facilitate a Corporate Circle.

CHAPTER 2

The Circle Model

For the great enemy of the truth is very often not the lie–deliberate, contrived and dishonest–but the myth–persistent, persuasive and unrealistic. ...We enjoy the comfort of opinions without the discomfort of thought.
— John F. Kennedy, commencement address at Yale University, June 11, 1962

Conflict is normal and all-pervasive. Although conflict can be productive, most often workplace conflict is destructive and can cause a ripple effect across an organization. Conflict is destructive because people often do not know how to diagnose it properly and if they do, are unable to fix it. Our inability to handle workplace disputes is linked to the following myths about conflict:

○ The dispute will blow over.

○ It's just one or two people.

○ Those involved just need to talk it out.

○ Emotions are dangerous.

○ We just need to control or remove the person responsible.

This chapter discusses these five myths, describes the three fundamental parts of Corporate Circles, and explains the origins of Circles.

Five Myths About Conflict

Myth 1. The dispute will blow over

Generally speaking we are not very good at figuring out the causes of many conflicts. This is not always our fault. The truth is that most conflict is difficult to diagnose, primarily because no one wants to admit to it or talk about it. Most people who are in a situation of conflict will do all they can to either avoid it or pretend it does not exist. When confronted, most people will say that everything is fine or that "things will blow over."

People go out of their way to avoid or ignore conflict because the majority of them think most conflict is caused by a difference of opinion or a difference in personality style that cannot be changed. They also think people will forget what happened in a conflict situation. This thinking is usually wrong.

Recall the famous saying: *People may forget what you said. They may forget what you did. But they will never forget how you made them feel.*

Although some conflict will go away, most conflict will merely go underground. Like a dormant volcano, unaddressed conflict can often cause eruptions in seemingly unrelated situations. And usually when you least suspect such an outburst.

These types of "eruptions" are simply symptoms of deeper problems that are causing disputes. If these problems are not brought to the surface and dealt with, they can lead to more disputes, stress, low morale, absenteeism and low productivity. These simmering conflicts are a major source of irritation for many organizations because they keep surfacing year after year.

> **Real life.** A few years ago I was asked to help Gary, an employee who had been in conflict with his co-workers for several months. Over the previous four years he had changed departments four times. He had a certain personality that seemed to irritate others easily. He was fiercely independent and one of the hardest workers in the company. However, Gary kept getting into minor disputes with his co-workers. A recent blowup with his manager was just another incident that, on its own, would not have been cause for concern. But together, this series of events caused what his colleagues began calling "a chilly work climate." Everyone assumed that Gary was just difficult to work with and that nothing could be done to solve the problem. The group held a Corporate Circle and

each person began to see how they were impacted by and contributing to what was going on. They created an action plan designed to prevent future conflict and were relived to have had the conversation.

In situations where there is ongoing or deep-seated conflict, no amount of prodding will evoke hidden feelings. The only way they will emerge is in a completely safe place where open conversation is promoted. Although a face-to-face meeting with a problem employee might seem like a quick fix, the power differential and work-related fears often cause people to clam up. The real story often stays hidden.

Myth 2. It's just one or two people

Many people think conflict is simply the fault of one person or a dispute between two people. Here are some statements one commonly hears when there is conflict:

- My boss is controlling.
- My staff is incompetent.
- My colleague is uncooperative.
- My assistant is impossible to manage.
- Jennifer and Jim just don't seem to get along.
- My manager never listens.

Notice that in each of these situations only one or two people are blamed for the problem.

In reality most conflict involves more than one or two people. Most conflict involves not only those who contribute to the conflict, but also those who are being impacted by the conflict.

When a situation is misdiagnosed as a dispute between two people, the wrong solution is usually selected. The solutions most recommended when there is conflict include conflict resolution training, conflict coaching, and supervisors privately to employees. Another common strategy is long-term performance management, with the hope that by clarifying expectations the conflict will fall away.

The main problem with most of these solutions is that they are based on one flawed assumption. It is usually assumed that *one or two people* are to blame for the conflict. On the basis of this assumption, the supervisor thinks that changing this person will address the problem. Unfortunately, fixing this single part of the problem usually does not cause the problem to go away, and conflict will often resurface later.

The reality of most organizational conflict is that several people are contributing, directly or indirectly, to the problem. Some are turning a blind eye, while others are actively supporting the situation. Often the manager or supervisor is one of those contributing, without recognizing it. I call this the sociology of workplace conflict.

This sociology is most apparent in situations of bullying or other power-related conflict. Through my work as a harassment investigator, I came to see that the "bully," although often responsible for much of the conflict, was actually being supported indirectly by the rest of the workplace.

My experiences were supported in a book titled *The Bully, the Bullied and the Bystander* by parenting and education guru Barbara Coloroso. Coloroso explains how each of the bully, the bullied and the bystanders play a particular role in determining what happens in a workplace. The bully is interested in maintaining control, usually through threats and power plays; the bullied is the victim who is the main target of the bully; and the bystanders consist of those who are hiding in fear from the bully and those who befriend the bully, usually in an attempt to avoid becoming the next one to be bullied.

> **Real life.** A few years ago, a local theatre company put on an interactive play about bullying in schools. The actors played out scenes where a bully attacked a classmate. The other actors played out the roles of the bystanders. At various points in the play, the director stopped the play and invited audience members to come onstage. The audience member was asked to play a character and to try their best to resolve the situation while in role. It came as a big surprise to the audience that none of the new cast members was able to shift the dynamics of the situation. Most surprising, however, was the way in which the other actors stayed in role and effectively interfered with the efforts of that new person to change the status quo. These actors were simply being true to their character and not consciously aware that they were still supporting the bullying.[again, interesting parallel]

Workplace conflict often mirrors school ground bullying, with "bystanders" contributing—even unconsciously—to the status quo. Given this social construction of workplaces, even removing the problem person does not necessarily improve the situation.

Myth 3. Those involved just need to talk it out

Many people think conflict can be resolved by bringing together the two people in apparent conflict to talk it out. In some organizations, a manager or a human resources person will assist them in having a conversation. Sometimes this works, but not usually. In many of these conversations people *cannot* or *will not* express what they are truly thinking or feeling.

Some people cannot find the words to describe how they are feeling or even what happened in a conflict. Often they are overwhelmed by emotions, especially fear that saying anything will only make matters worse. This is compounded by the fact that most people are unaware of many of the reasons why they behave as they do. They are often unable to access the deeper reasoning, explanations or motivations.

Even if they are able to articulate what went wrong, they will usually edit what they say to such an extent that true feelings are never expressed in a way that is useful for the other person to hear. Only rarely is the environment conducive to the promotion of an authentic conversation. Unless people feel safe, they will say only a fraction of what they are feeling. Most people fear repercussions from the other person or from their manager—whether justified or not. This fear is completely understandable but often misinterpreted by managers or those in a position of authority.

This can be witnessed in a court situation where a judge may try to settle a dispute and help the two parties come to an agreement. In this context the disputants rarely get to the root of the problem. Typically the two parties will argue about what they think they deserve, often through their lawyers. They may agree to settle or may agree to disagree. Usually only their two perspectives are brought to the table. Not only do the parties never really understand the other person's reasons for behaving as they did, they do not understand the impact of their actions on others. Worse yet, many walk away with even more hard feelings and resentment, particularly for not being acknowledged. Here is an example.

> **Real life.** In an episode of the real-life TV series *Judge Judy*, two parties were next-door-neighbors fighting over the cost of removing fallen leaves from one property. The parties argued heatedly about the fallen leaves—an event that had occurred over a year before. In the end Judge Judy decided that the leaves belonged to one neighbor and required that she pay for the cleanup. After the trial, when interviewed by the producers of the show, both parties were still angry and both vowed revenge! The real issue, which was probably respect, was never dealt with during the trial. The opportunity to heal the damage caused to the relationship and to help the neighbors begin to treat each other better was completely lost.

As most lawyers would agree, this mechanism is only marginally effective at resolving disputes and completely ineffective at transforming conflict into collaborative relationships.

This model has become acceptable mostly because of our adversarial systems and society. As a lawyer, I did not learn better ways to resolve disputes until about seven years into practice. Lawyers are not taught about the power of peers and community in resolving conflict. Take a look at the spectrum of dispute resolution methods below. None is designed to help the parties find common ground and reconnect. Indeed, these methods usually focus on differences and tend to divide the parties, even in family law situations.

- *Adjudication:* A judge decides on guilt and liability after weighing the evidence as presented by lawyers in a courtroom.

- *Arbitration:* An arbitrator selects a solution after listening to each of the people involved in the conflict.

- *Negotiation:* The parties negotiate an agreement, sometimes with negotiators. They tend to overstate their situation and mislead their opponent in order to gain ground.

- *Mediation:* A mediator helps those in conflict reach some sort of agreement. The mediator helps each person to articulate their position and underlying interests, and sometimes their emotions.

Although these methods help the parties come to an agreement, none is as specifically designed to transform conflict, enhance empathy or re-establish relationships. Although modern forms of mediation go much further, that is not generally their mandate.

In contrast, the main goal of a Corporate Circle is specifically to transform conflict and rebuild strong groups. In a Circle the whole group not only uncovers what is wrong but also decides how to make it better. There is no compromise or give and take. Instead there is the creation of a common understanding that results in a whole new way of seeing things and relating to each other. The focus is not on the dispute but on the beliefs and understandings that impact the way people treat each other. Conversations emphasize the things participants have in common and minimize the differences.

Myth 4. Emotions are dangerous

Conflict is typically rooted in hidden assumptions that people make about people and circumstances. Many of these assumptions are rooted in beliefs formed over time that are anchored in our emotions. Acknowledging these emotions is critical to resolving conflict.

Most dispute resolution methods try to ignore or separate out emotions because they are seen to be wild and destructive. As a result these methods uncover some of the underlying interests of the parties but do not tend to go deep enough. The disputants rarely get the opportunity to describe in an emotional way what is really bothering them—or what they feel is the source of the conflict. As a result they hold onto emotional baggage that will drive further disputes.

In their book *Transforming Conflict*, David Moore and John McDonald distinguish conflict from disputes. They describe disputes as factual differences and conflicts as "lingering states" that cause people to feel negatively about each other. Conflicts tend to involve several people and are usually caused by a set of assumptions that make people feel badly about others.

This interpretation explains why disputes can usually be resolved through a discussion or mediation whereas conflicts need to involve all those impacted by the conflict. Disputes can be resolved by agreeing on facts. Conflicts can only be resolved by agreeing on emotionally laden values. When resolving disputes, emotions can be separated out, but with conflict, the emotions are the root of the problem and must be exposed.

If conflict is resolved at only an intellectual level, in the short term people behave differently but will slowly be influenced by their hidden emotions that were not allowed to heal properly. Simply resolving a dispute between two individuals, who are mired in deeper workplace conflict, will not solve the problem. Problems including suspicion, ill-feeling and lack of trust will not likely dissipate until brought the surface.

Myth 5. We just need to control or remove the person responsible

Many people feel the only solution for dealing with conflict is to control, punish or remove the so-called offender.

In corporate situations, bad behavior is often seen as a violation of agreed-upon rules of the workplace. Most organizations operate within a basic, even if unwritten, code of conduct. This code describes how people should behave. Some rules relate to specific behaviors such as harassment and bullying.

Most of these corporate rules are based on a punitive-correction model. If an employee breaks one of the rules, he or she is punished. If it happens again, more serious punishments are imposed. When a person behaves badly, this person is seen to be completely at fault. In order to stop the so-called bad employee from harming others, he or she needs to be "straightened out."

This model assumes that this person is solely responsible and in control of the situation and that this person will correct his or her behavior if there are negative externally imposed consequences. It presumes that certain employees are bad and they need a hard lesson to make them good.

Our whole system of legal wrongful dismissal is based on this punitive-correction model. If an employee continues to break company rules, that employee must leave the company. The main problem with this model is that punishment usually does not work in workplaces—not for the individual, not for the organization, and not for society in general.

More often than not there are many reasons for the "bad" behavior. Rarely does a person intentionally and maliciously break a rule, and rarely does punishment address the problems facing most organizations.

Real life. I recall a situation in which one employee was continually late. She was subjected to progressive discipline and eventually was told that her job was on the line. As it turned out, the employee was a single parent and relied on her mother to take care of her children. Her mother rarely showed up on time in the morning. As a result, the woman missed her ride to work with her neighbor and had to take the bus. When she did this she was always late. She was too embarrassed to tell her supervisor and felt bad about letting her co-workers down. The penalties caused her to feel worse and even less inclined to speak to her supervisor. She felt trapped and did not know how to solve her problem. Luckily she disclosed this information before she lost her job and her supervisor agreed to accommodate her on these days.

One rarely knows exactly what is happening in people's lives. It is good practice to never assume too much. It may be that a worker who takes long lunch breaks is doing so to visit his dying mother at the hospital. Some of the thoughts to keep in mind when conducting Corporate Circles are the following:

○ All people are human and deserving of respect, no matter what they have done.

○ Every human wants to feel free and to have choices.

○ Reality is subjective, and every person has many different perspectives.

○ Peers, co-workers and supervisors have enormous influence on how people behave.

○ The workplace community is a complex web of relationships that reinforce behaviors.

The punitive-correction model is condemned in modern child-rearing books. Punishment is seen as an archaic means of discipline. According to research, if you punish a child, the child may obey you in the short term but will most likely grow to dislike you and not respect you. Children will avoid a hurtful situation but will rarely learn the proper behavior. As a result they will tend to behave in similar ways or lash out in different contexts. Have you ever liked someone who punished you? Have you ever felt a desire to improve after being punished?

Here are some modern parenting rules reflected in the model of Corporate Circles:

○ You may have done something inappropriate (focus on behavior).

○ You are not a bad person (bolster self-esteem).

○ We need to reconnect you to the group on the basis of shared values.

Of course, punishment still gets used in corporations, as it does in some families. Changing the paradigm will take generations. But the results are not always those anticipated. Here are some of the things I have learned about punishment as used in corporations:

○ People who behave badly, if punished, do not necessarily behave better.

○ If a person learns about how his behavior has impacted others, that person will be less likely to repeat the behavior.

○ If a person is allowed to remedy the problem, she is more likely to feel hopeful for the future and is more open to repairing relationships.

○ If a person is involved in finding a solution, he is more likely to follow through on that solution.

The cost of a punitive-correction model is that it instills fear in everyone. In such an environment, even the best employees often live in fear of punishment. Fearful employees translate into unhappy and underproductive employees. This model is simply inadequate at producing a workplace culture that supports human or organizational growth. In short, *why would you harm people who harm people to teach people that harming people is wrong?*

The desired outcome in the wake of conflict, which is a natural outcome of a Corporate Circle, is a shift in behavior of the person "causing" the harm and others who might be contributing, permitting the "offender" to redeem himself and thus reestablish healthy relationships.

A Deeper Understanding of Conflict

The five common myths people have about conflict teach us the following:

- ○ Conflict will not usually go away on its own.
- ○ Conflict is rarely just a factual dispute.
- ○ Hidden feelings drive most conflict.
- ○ Conflict usually involves several people.
- ○ Many people are impacted by conflict (the ripple effect).
- ○ Punishment does not work to transform conflict or enhance empathy.

This deeper understanding of conflict forms the foundation of Corporate Circles. If you see conflict in this way, then three things must happen. Those involved in and impacted by the conflict must do the following:

1. Diagnose the problem and uncover the hidden causes;

2. Come to a shared understanding about what happened; and

3. Together create a solution.

These are the three fundamental facets of Corporate Circles. In order for these three things to happen, any Circle process must ensure that people feel safe to talk and express their emotions. This safety is integral to the success of the Circle process. Chapter 3 provides details on how to create this safe place.

In a Corporate Circle a whole group gets together to have a candid conversation. All those who are impacted are brought together. The Circle provides a safe environment in which each person can share their perspectives on what has been happening in the workplace and, more importantly, how to move on.

Origins of Corporate Circles

Corporate Circles are based on a combination of models and practices including restorative practices, dialogue and appreciative inquiry. For resources on which this conflict resolution model is based, see the list of references at the back of this book.

Corporate Circles have their roots in process called conferencing that was first used in criminal law in the early 1970s. Conferencing was based on principles of restorative justice—or restoring, rather than punishing, offenders.

In the early seventies several groups in Canada, New Zealand and Australia who dealt with juvenile crimes felt that a better solution than prison was a peer- and community-based process. They found that when the perpetrator and the victims faced each other and shared their perspectives, the conflict was transformed.

According to one history, the idea of restorative justice began in the small town of Elmira, Ontario, Canada. In 1974 two young men got drunk and vandalized several properties.

They were caught and convicted. The probation officer Mark Yanzi, who was responsible for the sentencing report, wanted to come up with an innovative sentencing solution, so he canvassed an informal group of criminal justice volunteers and professionals who met regularly. He felt that the best thing for the young offenders was to have them meet their victims. He was able to convince the judge, who ordered the two men to meet with the victims, report on the damage suffered, and negotiate a settlement. When the young offenders and the victims faced each other and shared their perspectives, the conflict was transformed, and the parties worked together to remedy the situation.

The conferencing process has expanded around the world with the help of Real Justice, a non-profit organization dedicated to promoting conferencing and other restorative practices. In his book *Conferencing Handbook*, Terry O'Connell describes conferencing as emerging in New Zealand in 1989 when the government introduced a process called family group conferencing. A conference was held in cases of juvenile offences that brought together the extended family of a youth to develop a plan and come up with a solution.

Slowly research began to emerge demonstrating the value and impact of these processes. Much of the effectiveness of the model is based on Silvan Tomkins's theory of human effect or emotions as described by Donald Nathanson (1992). Conferencing allows for the free expression of emotions, which allows healing while minimizing negative impacts.

Howard Zehr in *Changing Lenses: A New Focus for Crime and Justice* (1990) describes how restorative justice differs from the current justice system in that it does not punish, blame or shame a person for committing a crime. It involves offenders in the justice system and makes them accountable for their actions to those who have been impacted. It allows for the offender to apologize and make things right. This model is best described in the previously mentioned book by David Moore and John MacDonald, *Transforming Conflict*.

Restorative processes are used by many groups for several purposes. Quakers, native groups and Mennonites use restorative practices in their day-to-day operations. Schools use circles to deal with bullying and inappropriate behavior. Restorative processes were used in South Africa under the guidance of Nelson Mandela as victims of apartheid told their stories through the Truth and Reconciliation Commission. Finally, companies such as Roca Inc., a non profit organization based in Minnesota introduced the concept of circles throughout their entire organization. These circles included conflict circles, management circles and ideas circles, all designed to enhance communication and build stronger working groups.

The concept of Circles is an ancient one with many applications, and Corporate Circles integrate this proven model into an organizational setting. Read on to learn how to prepare for, create and facilitate a Corporate Circle in your workplace.

CHAPTER 3

How to Create a Corporate Circle

You can only hope to find a lasting solution to a conflict if you have learned to see the other [person] objectively, but at the same time, to experience his difficulties subjectively.

— Dag Hammarskjold

The main goal of any Corporate Circle is to have an authentic conversation. Through this conversation the group will be able to transform conflict and build trusting relations. To create this type of conversation you need four things: the right people, the right place, the right process and the proper principles—the four Ps. In other words, you want to do the following:

○ include the right mix of *people*

    ○ create a safe *place* or environment

    ○ adopt a *process* that supports full participation

    ○ adhere to *principles* that ensure authentic dialogue

This chapter explains how you can achieve the four Ps within your organization. It guides you through the fundamental steps that will guarantee a successful Circle.

Include the Right Mix of People

A Circle will unfold naturally when the right mix of people is included. If you include too few people, the conversation will be slow and seem more like individual monologues than a dialogue. This often happens in mediations that involve only two people. If you include too many people, several people will not have the opportunity to contribute.

If you include the wrong people, such as those who are not impacted by the conflict, those who wield power over a group or those who might sabotage the group, the conversation will be stilted and in some cases superficial. If you include only those who agree with each other, not much new will be uncovered.

In situations of workplace conflict or poor group relations, the right mix consists of those people who are most impacted by the situation. This means both those who may be the cause of the problem and those who may be contributing to the problem. But equally important are those who may be avoiding the problem, even though they are bothered by it.

Rarely does a situation of corporate conflict involve only

two people. Here is a quick checklist of people to consider inviting to the Circle:

- people who are directly involved in a conflict

- those who have been identified as causing a problem

- those who are most bothered by the conflict

- those who are trying to ignore the conflict or hoping it will go away

- managers who have had similar problems previously

- people in other departments who come into contact with the group in conflict

- human resources people who have tried to resolve a conflict

- family members who are frustrated by the conflict

In order to have a fruitful conversation and to obtain a long-term solution, many of these people need to be involved.

When narrowing the list of who to include, keep in mind one of the main functions of a Corporate Circle—to create a common understanding about what is happening. This common understanding emerges as each participant contributes their piece of the picture. Like a jigsaw puzzle, if a piece is missing, the picture looks different.

This common understanding is the thing that helps the group make sense of what happened and understand how they got there. It also helps the group prevent the situation from occurring again and helps them move forward. During a successful Corporate Circle each person should be able to:

- share their perspective and contribute to the common understanding
- vent or unburden themselves of any pent-up bad feelings and resentment
- connect on a human level and thus build empathy and trust
- repair any fractured relations and reestablish lines of communication

There is a real danger to not including the right mix. Barbara Coloroso, in her book, *The Bully, the Bullied and the Bystander*, identified the network of relationships that support bullying behavior. Her research indicates that many people in schools as well as in workplaces support the status quo by simply saying nothing or refusing to intervene. The so-called bystanders play a significant role in keeping the bully in a position of power.

In my experience, there is a tendency to want to keep the size of the group small and to keep a situation contained. However, the reality is that even the smallest conflict has a huge ripple effect. It impacts many parts of the organization, customers, suppliers and even competitors. By limiting the Circle to include only some of those impacted, its long-term effectiveness will be compromised. A Circle is an ideal way to get rid of suppressed anger, frustration or resentment.

Create a Safe Place or Environment

The key to any successful Circle is the creation of a safe place. It is this safe environment that allows individuals to become open enough to share their perspectives on what has been happening. Without a safe space, there will be no conversation. A safe place consists of both the physical location and the psychological atmosphere.

A safe physical place is a neutral, quiet and confidential room. A boardroom, conference room or meeting room is usually fine. It should not be a room in which the group usually gathers or conducts business. It is best to have it away from where the group works—such as in a nearby hotel or in a separate building. The best way to find out whether a room is appropriate is to ask the participants.

The room should hold the group comfortably without being too big or too small. If there are fifteen people there must be space to place fifteen chairs in a circle facing each other. It is a good idea to have space at the back of the room where participants can mingle before and after the Circle and have coffee breaks, so people do not leave the room and enter into separate conversations.

The room must be closed to outsiders and there can be no interruptions.

> **Real life.** A few years ago I conducted a Corporate Circle in a boardroom on a floor separate from where a twelve-person team worked. I posted a notice on the main door of the boardroom stating that a meeting was in progress that should not be disturbed. The

Circle was interrupted two times. At one point a woman from another department walked in through a side door to set up coffee. When she first walked in, the conversation abruptly stopped. I stood up and spoke to her in private about the need to keep this meeting completely confidential. Later, another person walked in without knocking to set up lunch. I spoke to her as well and she left immediately. A few days after the Circle I received a phone call from one of the participants. She was concerned that others knew about what had happened in the Circle. She thought that the two women who came into the room had listened to what was being said.

This situation is a good reminder of how sensitive people are to the issue of confidentiality and how important it is to anticipate the ways in which confidentiality of a Circle could be compromised.

As mentioned, in addition to creating a safe physical space is the need to establish a safe psychological space. Those who do not *feel* safe will simply not participate.

Since every one of us feels differently about safety and since a sense of safety is dependent on so many factors, it is always best to start from the position that in any situation of conflict, no one feels particularly safe.

Real life. I often ask audiences in workshops to describe how safe they feel on a scale from one to ten. Ten is the safest and one is the least safe. An example of a ten might be lying in bed early in the morning with a duvet pulled up to your chin. A one might be hanging by your fingers from a cliff above a shallow river. Most people sitting in an audience feel about eight on this scale. A few people might feel like a ten—until I start walking toward them. As you can see, as I move closer this person's sense of safety will decline. This person's sense of safety shifts significantly with a small change in circumstances in a matter of moments.

Each person in a Circle will feel more or less safe depending on many factors including personal disposition, who is in the room, past relationships, what happened the evening before, and so on. You should never assume that just because you feel safe, others will too. Here is a list of factors that add to or detract from the psychological safety of a group:

- ○ the predictability of what will happen in the Circle
- ○ the level of participation in the conversation
- ○ the voice and demeanor of the facilitator
- ○ amount of time spent in the room and in one chair
- ○ the emotional tone of the conversation
- ○ the extent to which one person controls the conversation

The more that participants know in advance about what will happen in the Circle, the safer they will feel on arrival. The more that people participate in the conversation, the safer the group will feel. The safer that people feel, the more they will be willing to contribute, and so it goes.

The important thing is to be aware of how participants

are feeling, how the group is feeling as a whole, and how you are feeling as facilitator. Watch for clues such as body language and "loaded" words to gauge the emotional temperature of the group. Obvious clues that participants are feeling unsafe or uncooperative include people crossing their arms in front of their chests and leaning away from the group. More subtle clues that participants may be feeling safe and connected include a sense of relaxation and increased participation.

Adopt a Process that Supports Full Participation

The process used in a Circle must, of course, support full participation. To ensure this happens, attendance in the Circle must be voluntary. Each person must be allowed time to speak and there must be a common focus.

Each person must be invited and be told that they have the option to not attend. No one can be forced to attend. Although this voluntary attendance might be a problem in other conflict resolution processes, it is not usually a problem for Corporate Circles. As long as a core number of those impacted by the conflict attend, it may not matter if one or two people do not come. Having said this, the conversation will definitely be different.

Remind those who are hesitant to attend that participating in a Circle is an opportunity to hear what others feel but, more importantly, it is also an opportunity to tell their side of the story—which is often unknown by others.

Many conflicts are related to power imbalances. Therefore, equality is a critical aspect of Corporate Circles. The circle itself is a shape that ensures that no one has a position of more power than any other person.

This sense of equality must be reflected in the conversation by allowing each person an opportunity to participate. This does not mean that everyone must participate. Indeed, there is no need for everyone to participate, and participants may stay silent if they wish. However, after the Circle process is complete, each person must feel as if they had the opportunity to speak.

The Circle process creates a space where participants feel compelled to communicate in a respectful way. Therefore it is not necessary to ask participants to speak or listen in any particular way. Indeed, to interfere with the natural flow of communication and the natural expression of feelings can lessen the chance of having a deeper conversation. Participants should not be editing what they might be feeling.

In situations of heated conversation, the Circle has a funny way of adjusting when things have gone too far. Usually one or two participants will act in ways that bring the Circle back into balance. It is quite remarkable to watch as a group reestablishes the safety of the Circle.

Real life. I recall one Circle in which a man kept making light of what had been happening in the workplace. There had been serious allegations of bullying, harassment and violence between employees. As each person raised a concern he would make a joke about the situation or a person. I recall he atmosphere feeling like an elevator ride. The conversation would go up as people told their stories and shared their perspectives and then drop down when the joke was told. Up then down. Eventually the ups out numbered the downs and the group began to have a more meaningful conversation. The joking employee slowly refrained from joking during this conversation without being addressed directly by me or by anyone in the group.

The Circle must focus on one or two issues for several reasons. First, there is not enough time to deal with more than one or two issues to the extent required to get to the root of the problem. Second, a single issue actually pulls the group together to focus on resolving something specific.

The ideal situation is when there has been one triggering event that caused a conflict. Each person has their own perspective on what happened, but after hearing from others in the Circle, participants quickly learn that there are many shades to the truth and that they are all impacted by the conflict in unique ways. In learning this, they will feel that they have accomplished something by the end of the Circle and not increased their level of frustration.

Adhere to Principles that Ensure Authentic Dialogue

Two basic principles of any Circle are confidentiality and transparency. Confidentiality means that whatever is said during the Corporate Circle must not leave that Circle. This is obviously important for providing safety, but also important for those outside the Circle, such as managers. These outsiders need to know that they will not find out what happened in the Circle unless everyone in the Circle agrees to tell them.

Maintaining confidentiality can prove difficult in many workplaces, since it is difficult to keep anything secret. Therefore it is accepted that some things might slip out in conversation, but everyone must agree before participating that they will keep everything confidential, to the best of their ability. Often Circle participants will agree to give the supervisor a copy of the final agreement or may offer a short statement from the group about where they wish to go from here.

The second fundamental principle of a Corporate Circle is transparency. One of the main reasons why conflict endures is because people simply stop talking. They stop talking because they are afraid. They are afraid to share with others because they are angry or frustrated and think any conversation might make matters worse. In essence, they are not sure how they will be interpreted or whether the information might be shared with others.

This is why transparency in the Circle process is so important. Deep conflict can make people become suspicious of *any* process—particularly if other processes have been tried and failed.

To ensure transparency, every person must be told the same thing. They must also be told that the facilitator is telling everyone the same thing. Each person must be able to ask any question about the process, and no part of the process should be secret in any way. No person should be treated differently than any other person. The best way to ensure this consistency is to provide each person with a one-page description of the process, then discuss this page in detail with each participant before interviewing that person.

Although the Circle process has some key principles or "rules," the process must also remain flexible. By being well versed in the principles, a facilitator will know when flexibility is possible. If the process is too rigid, the participants will feel hampered. However, to ensure consistency and fairness, keep in mind that any change to the process must be shared with the others and explained to them.

The Outcome is to Achieve Consensus

Most people do not believe in consensus because their personal experiences have shown them the difficulty in getting everyone to agree. In most corporate meetings, one or two people will not agree, which can make consensus impossible.

This inability to reach consensus—the hallmark of most corporate meetings—does not and should not happen in a Circle. If the process is effective, each person will reach a shared understanding of the problem and feel a shared responsibility for resolving the conflict. The group itself finds its own unique way to ensure that each person agrees with the ultimate outcome. If a person does not agree, this is a sign that something more needs to be discussed, and the conversation will continue – either in this Circle or in a follow up Circle.

Once you know who to invite, how to create a safe place, how to use a process that supports full participation and what principles to adhere to, you are ready to begin your preparations for the Circle.

CHAPTER 4

How to Prepare for a Corporate Circle

One of the easiest human acts is also the most healing. Listening to someone. Simply listening. Not advising or coaching but silently and fully listening.

— Margaret Wheatley, Turning to One Another

Listening is a form of accepting.

—Stella Terrill Mann

Once you understand the basic principles behind Corporate Circles and know how to create one, you are ready to begin your preparation. This chapter outlines how to do the following as you prepare to hold your Corporate Circle:

- determine suitability
- select the timing
- ensure people are available
- select a date and organize other logistics

After preparing for the Corporate Circle you will need to interview each of the possible participants, select the actual participants and design a seating plan. These steps are discussed in the next chapter.

Determine Suitability

There are many factors to consider when deciding whether a Corporate Circle is appropriate in your particular situation. The following list poses some of the questions you need to ask at this stage.

- Is there a conflict, and not just a factual dispute?
- Are there several people impacted by the conflict?
- Are there more than a few people contributing to the dispute?
- Are there hidden causes of the conflict?
- Do you want to restore the workplace, rather than punish someone?
- Does the problem involve feelings or emotions?
- Would you like everyone in the group to contribute to a solution?

If you have answered yes to most of the questions above, then a Corporate Circle is probably appropriate for your situation.

Corporate Circles are most beneficial in situations where one or more of the following conditions occur:

- bullying or harassment

- abuse of power

- continual disputes over time

- discrimination and general mistreatment

- slow simmering conflict

- damaged workplace relations

Corporate Circles are also beneficial in a situation where there are newly combined corporate cultures. They are especially helpful when an organization wants to repair harm or heal internal relations after a negative event.

Select the Timing

In addition to being suitable, the situation must also be ripe for intervention. This means that the individuals affected must be ready to have a conversation. There must be a reason to hold the circle, either to resolve conflict or to build stronger relations. Although a Corporate Circle can be used at any time, they tend to be most effective when there is a strong need and motivation.

The most common reason, unfortunately, is desperation. Often corporate groups endure conflict for a long time. They will ignore it, try to talk it away, try and try to train it away. Because circles are fairly new on the corporate scene, most groups first try more traditional techniques, like performance reviews, mediation or training. I am often asked to hold a Circle as a last resort. In these situations the group might have been through a fact-finding process or formal investigation that found no clear person to blame or assigned no clear guilt. A group may have exhausted all the corporate remedial policies and may be at a loss as to what to do next. Often groups are at their wits' end.

This is good and bad. It is good because they will be ready to try anything, but it is bad because they will have been through so many different processes that they may be cynical, not to mention exhausted. At the other end of the spectrum there is no clear conflict, but simply a real desire on the part of a few to build stronger relations or reestablish commitment to the group. This is not just a proactive use of the Corporate Circles, but a way of establishing trust and team building.

In both these situations there is usually a serious motivating factor or event that urges the group to hold a Circle and it is these very same factors that make it so difficult for the group to meet and talk.

Situations of conflict and team building are often accompanied by anxiety and these feelings evoke fear which causes people to stop communicating. This results in less more negative assumptions causing people to avoid *any* form of communication. It feels too dangerous to them. This reaction is completely natural, and indeed this is why providing a safe place to communicate in a Circle is so effective at reestablishing relations. As for timing however, these circumstances often cause issue to go without resolution for a long time.

It is rare to find a situation when everyone in a group wants to have a conversation. More typically, people in conflict want to get rid of the conflict and are willing to do what it takes to make matters better. They may not be looking forward to it, but are willing to take the chance in spite of their reservations.

The timing will not be right if the necessary participants are not available to attend. This can happen when people are absent or refuse to come. Although every person impacted does not need to attend, there are certain people in each situation whose attendance would result in a more meaningful conversation. Many of the fears people have about having a conversation are dispelled once participants learn about the Circle process and the key component of providing a safe place to *have* the conversation.

Another timing issue relates to any other processes that may be taking place at the same time, such as litigation or formal grievances. Since a Corporate Circle involves uncovering ideas and opinions, those processes might be compromised if a Circle is not timed properly.

> **Real life.** I was asked to conduct a Corporate Circle in a large corporation for about thirty employees and managers. One of the senior executives had been removed from the workplace in secrecy. There were rumors of sexual harassment, and several employees knew that criminal charges that had been laid

against the executive. There were also rumors that the executive had filed a wrongful dismissal claim against the corporation. Lawyers for the organization had spoken to almost every employee but had not told them what was happening. Even though there were two court procedures in the works, which were not likely to be resolved soon, I was hired to help the employees heal from the experience, develop a respectful workplace and get back to enjoying their jobs. And it worked.

As you can see, it is important to keep other processes separate from the Corporate Circle and ensure the confidentiality of each so that no process is compromised by any other. Sometimes it is best to put off the Circle until the other processes have been completed. Sometimes it is best to go ahead with the Circle, for it may cause some of the other proceedings to fall away or get settled.

In terms of other proceedings, it is important to remain open to other ways to resolve the conflict. For example, there may be a company policy or collective agreement that provides a process for resolving these types of conflicts. Many company policies include harassment and bullying rules and remedies. Most of these policies, however, are based on the punishment model, so are most effective when one person is clearly at fault and needs to be handled apart from the other workers.

Before beginning the Circle process, you will want to find out what has transpired beforehand to resolve the current situation. In most cases something has been attempted, even if it is just training. You will want to know whether managers, human resources personnel or the legal department has been involved. In some situations, a "fact finding" will already have been conducted to find out what process is most appropriate for the situation.

To remain neutral, however, the facilitator should not learn about the situation from any source except from the participants. A facilitator need not look at anything before speaking to the participants. This is particularly important to the perceived neutrality of the facilitator. Participants might be less inclined to speak candidly if they know that the facilitator has already gathered information about the circumstances. The Circle facilitator should go into the process completely "clean."

Ensure People are Available

The ideal Circle is one that has all the "critical" people in attendance. Who these are is described in detail in chapter 3, but essentially include the following:

- those who are most directly impacted by the conflict

- those who need to share their perspective

- those who can contribute to the solution

The fewer "critical" people able to attend, the less effective the Circle will be.

However, not everyone needs to be there. For example, if a workplace "bully" is absent from a Corporate Circle, the Circle will still be effective. What transpires will be useful for the rest of the employees. They will be able to describe how the behavior has impacted each of them and can suggest solutions. The Circle will also have an indirect impact on the whole workplace and the bullying situation, since the employees will gain a new common understanding about what is actually happening and will create a mutual solution. The absent "bully" will not know what transpired in the Circle and will have lost the opportunity to share his or her perspective and perhaps apologize. Although this might temporarily alienate the "bully" the others will respond differently to this person in light of their new knowledge and the situation will necessarily change.

Having said that, if you do not have a core group of people available to attend, it is best to postpone the Circle. For example, some employees may have left the department or the company. Some may be on temporary or long-term leave. Some may be on holiday, on sabbatical or have been temporary relocated. In some situations, individuals may simply not want to participate, but may not be entirely candid about this and may sabotage efforts to hold the Circle.

> **Real life.** I met with a large executive board to discuss the possibility of holding a Circle. The chair explained to me that the board was in serious and continuous conflict and that they had tried everything—from training to setting strict rules of procedure for their meetings. I was told by the chair that something dramatic had to be done. I spoke to the board as a whole and explained the Circle process. The board went away, held a secret vote and unanimously decided

to hold a Corporate Circle. Then the problems began. I began phoning executives to set up interviews. I was politely told (usually by their assistants) that each executive had no dates available in the near future. After hearing this from several board members, I phoned the chair and suggested that the timing was not right.

Unless the participants see some value in having a conversation, holding a Circle can be a waste of time. Also, if several key people do not want to attend, there is also a high likelihood that they will cancel at the last minute, causing inconvenience for the others. That's why it's important to get "buy-in" and commitment from the potential participants. (The next chapter explains how to do this.)

Related to availability is the psychological state of the participants. Some individuals may not benefit from participating in a Circle or may become distressed in process. This is where significant judgment and intuition on the part of the facilitator is required. If a person shows signs of trauma, abuse, mental illness, or alcoholism special care must be taken. It is always best in these circumstances to consult and expert before engaging these individuals in the Circle process.

Select a Date and Organize Other Logistics

The final step in preparation is the logistical details. Here is a short list:

- *Select a date and time.* A Corporate Circle including ten to fifteen people will take about five hours. It will rarely take less than three hours, no matter what size the group.

- *Book a room.* The room you choose should be completely private and soundproof. No interruptions should be permitted. It's a good idea to have an open area at the back of the room or a waiting room just outside where participants can mingle before and after the Circle.

- *Inform participants.* It is best to prepare a detailed memo to go to all participants. You will find a sample memo at the end of this chapter.

- *Arrange for refreshments.* It is ideal to have refreshments before, during and after the Circle. Coffee or teas at the start can help make the atmosphere more inviting and relaxed, and snacks can help keep energy levels high. The final refreshments allow the group to come together as a group again, outside the Circle. This final refreshment is very important for completing the process.

- *Locate a support number.* Always provide participants with a phone number of a support person such as an employee assistance person who they can call for emotional support if need be. Some people like to know there is someone to speak to in case issues get raised that are not worked out during the Circle. It is also useful to bring tissue to the Circle.

Once you have made these arrangements you will be able to hold the preliminary meetings with the potential participants. The way in which you prepare the participants is described in the next chapter.

CHECKLIST: How to Prepare for a Corporate Circle

Step 1. Determine suitability

- ☐ Is there a conflict, and not just a factual dispute?
- ☐ Are there several people impacted by the conflict?
- ☐ Are there more than a few people contributing to the dispute?
- ☐ Are there hidden causes of the conflict?
- ☐ Do you want to restore the workplace, rather than punish someone?
- ☐ Does the problem involve feelings or emotions?
- ☐ Would you like everyone in the group to contribute to a solution?

Step 2. Select the timing

- ☐ Is the group ready?
- ☐ Is there a conflict or a real desire to build relations?
- ☐ What has been done so far?
- ☐ Are any formal procedures happening now?

Step 3. Ensure people are available

- ☐ Put together a list of participants
- ☐ Are all "critical" people available?

Step 4. Set a date and organize other logistics
- ☐ Select a date and time
- ☐ Book a room
- ☐ Inform participants
- ☐ Arrange for refreshments
- ☐ Locate a support number

SAMPLE: Memorandum to Possible Participants

To: [The Department]
From: [The Department Head/Human Resources Person]
Date: [Date]
Re: Corporate Circle

Over the past few months this department has been considering ways to improve working relations and enhance the workplace environment.

[Authorizing office] has agreed to hold a Corporate Circle for this department. It will be held on [date] from [time] to [time] in [location]. This Corporate Circle will provide an opportunity to discuss workplace issues and consider ways to improve communication and relationships. A handout titled *Corporate Circles at a Glance* is attached. (see chapter 1)

The facilitator, [name], will be meeting with you individually over the next few weeks to discuss the process and some of your personal concerns. In the meantime, if you have any questions, please feel free to speak to me. All information will be held in strictest confidence.

Chapter 5

How to Prepare Circle Participants

The origin of all conflict between me and my fellow men is that I do not say what I mean, and that I do not do what I say. For this confuses the poisons… the situation between myself and the other. By our contradiction, our lie, we foster conflict situations and give them power over us until they enslave us.

— Martin Buber, the Way of Man

Once you have determined suitability, decided on timing, and ensured people are available, you will want to prepare each of the possible participants. This involves meeting with each person individually for at least an hour. The general format of the meeting is as follows:

- introduce yourself and discuss confidentiality

- describe the Corporate Circle process

○ answer questions about the process

○ discuss participant's hopes and expectations

○ describe what happens next

This meeting is critical to the Circle process for a number of reasons. Unlike other meetings, the Circle one-on-one meetings are *not* for gathering information. They are not interviews. In fact, the facilitator does not need to write down anything that is said. The main purpose of the meeting is to begin the Circle process. This means the facilitator must do the following:

○ prepare participants for what will happen in the Circle

○ help participants articulate facts, thoughts and feelings

○ help participants contemplate other perspectives

○ identify key events or issues for the Circle

○ seek informed consent

After completing the meetings, you will be able to select and invite those who will attend the Circle. You will then design a seating plan and select the first speaker.

Prepare Participants for What Will Happen

All those who attend the Circle must be spoken to beforehand, even if over the telephone. This meeting should last for at least one hour. The importance of this conversation cannot be overstated.

Real life. I was asked to hold a Corporate Circle in another city. I had arranged the one-on-one meetings so that they could all be held in the two days prior to the Circle. At the last minute, one of the participants canceled her meeting and told me that she would call me the evening before the Circle. She called at about ten at night and in a sleepy voice told me that she really had nothing to add. I walked her through the Circle process, but she was simply unable to have a conversation. The next day in the Circle it was apparent that she felt out of place. It was not until our break, after two hours in conversation, that she came to me concerned about what was going on. After the Circle, she told me that she regretted not having met with me beforehand and was sorry she had been cynical about the process.

I learned several lessons from this. Some people may not embrace the process, so the facilitator must let the participants decide if they wish to have a one-on-one meeting. If they refuse to have a meeting, I do not invite them to the Circle. If they are not properly prepared, the process is not effective for them, and their unpreparedness is not fair to the others in the Circle.

As for the meeting, it is always best to start out slowly. Ask questions about the person and their job, such as job title, job responsibilities, work group members and who they report to. The conversation goes something like this:

Hi, I am Maureen Fitzgerald. I will be facilitating the Corporate Circle next week. During this hour I will tell you a bit about me and the Corporate Circle process. I will then allow you to tell me a little bit about what has been happening for you recently in the workplace.

Everything you say to me is confidential. I will not share it with anyone and will not mention it in the Circle. I would like you to keep this conversation confidential as well.

As for me, I am a lawyer and expert in conflict and collaboration. I have practiced law for over fifteen years and now devote my time to helping organizations prevent conflict and build strong teams. Although I am a lawyer, I am not acting in my legal capacity and not providing any legal advice.

I will be meeting with those involved and impacted by the conflict. This will include all immediate staff and may include others outside the workplace. I will hold one Corporate Circle on [date] for about three to five hours. Although I decide who to invite, I welcome your input.

During the Corporate Circle we will share opinions and feelings about what has been happening in the workplace. Specifically, I will ask what has been happening, how to repair any harm and how to prevent further conflict. Each person will be given an opportunity to speak openly and candidly and is invited to explain the impact of the events at a personal and professional level. At the end of the Circle you will each canvass ideas about how to move forward and will draft an action plan to take away. It will be disclosed to others only to the extent the group wishes.

My role is to facilitate the discussion and help the group to consider solutions while keeping the conversation on track. The ultimate goal is to transform the conflict into more positive working relations.

The only requirement is that you meet with me now and stay in the Circle until it is over. If you have any questions after this meeting, please phone me. It is best you speak to me before speaking to others in your group.

I usually provide something in writing at the first meeting that describes the Circle process so the potential participant has something to review. A sample memorandum to Circle participants appears at the end of this chapter.

Sometimes it is useful to walk participants through what will happen on the day of the Circle. For example, you might say:

When you walk into the boardroom next Tuesday, coffee will be available. I will seat everyone in the Circle, then I will begin the conversation. I will have asked someone previously to speak first. You can speak or choose not to. You will not be required to say anything. I will speak only rarely, to stimulate the conversation.

Depending on the participant's personality and their involvement in the conflict, you may also want to mention that emotions may surface. Some of the common emotions are anger, surprise, embarrassment, vulnerability and regret. You can explain that participants may move in and out of these emotional states as the conversation progresses, ultimately moving to a state of understanding.

Help Participants Articulate Facts, Thoughts and Feelings

The Circle process actually begins in the individual meetings, well before the actual event. This is because as people begin to tell their stories about what has been happening for them, they begin to process what has happened and begin to see different perspectives. They are often surprised when they begin to put their thoughts and feelings into words. This articulation helps them reflect on the events and helps them to understand their own and others' roles.

The easiest way to help people articulate their thoughts and feelings is by simply allowing them to tell their story. There can be absolutely no judgment on the part of the facilitator, because every story is true to each person. These stories are critical because they are directing their current behavior.

At this stage it is best to ask open-ended questions such as the following:

- Tell me what has been happening.

- How do you see the situation?

- How have things been for you?

- Who has been affected?

- What is your interest in resolving this?

- Who do you think should attend the Circle?

- How did you feel then?

- How do you feel now?

Silence and echoing are useful techniques that subtly encourage the participant to continue speaking. Paraphrasing should be avoided, since you do not want to reword what the person is saying or speed up their thought process. The facilitator must allow each person to find their own words to bring to the Circle.

As each person talks about what has been happening, they begin to untangle any confused thoughts and begin to reflect on the feelings they had at the time as well as the feelings they now hold. If the meeting is effective, participants will feel safe enough to release some of the feelings they may have been holding inside. This initial venting of emotions results in a number of positive effects both during the meeting and during the Circle. These effects include:

- a sense of being heard

- a sense of relief that something is being done

- ○ a release of pent-up anxiety or emotional baggage

- ○ a new understanding about how the problem has been impacting them

- ○ a sense of trust and belief in the Circle process

It is absolutely critical that the facilitator not react negatively to anything that is said. An nonjudgmental attitude will encourage the person being interviewed to continue talking and build a sense of trust and confidence in the facilitator. This will enhance a sense of safety and reassurance that they will not be judged in the Circle.

By the end of the meeting each person should have been able to acknowledge that there is a conflict and that they have been impacted by it. This is very important. They should be able to recognize that certain events may have been catalysts. They should have a sense of what they need to say in the Circle.

Help Participants Contemplate Other Perspectives

Before, during and after the pre-Circle meetings, each individual will be thinking about what happened in the workplace and what happened to precipitate the conflict. Often during this time they will try to recall what happened and provide theories and formulate explanations. These thoughts emerge on their own in isolation, usually without the benefit of hearing from others.

The meeting is a good time to discuss and in some cases challenge these thoughts, not because they are wrong, but rather because these thoughts will usually be challenged to some degree in the Circle. By challenging these thoughts the facilitator does two things: prepare the participants for the Circle conversation but also allow them to consider the possibility of different perspectives. If you do this well, the person will not be as surprised during the Circle and will be more open to listening when others are describing their perspectives.

Here are some sample questions to encourage participants to consider other perspectives:

- o   Is there another way of looking at the situation?
- o   Is there another way of making sense of that?
- o   Is it possible that someone might have seen it differently?
- o   How might you have done things differently?
- o   What else could have been motivating that person?

All those invited to the Circle have some role in the conflict, either directly or indirectly. During the one-on-one meeting it is helpful to explain this and allow the person to explore their role.

Identify Key Events and Issues for the Circle

During the meetings with the potential participants, the facilitator will begin to form a clearer picture about what has been going on in the department or in the organization. This will enable you to do three specific tasks:

- o identify those who were impacted by the conflict and thus better determine who to invite to the Circle

- o identify three or four catalysts of conflict that can be addressed in the Circle

- o identify the key contributors to the conflict, enabling you to select a person to begin the Circle conversation, if necessary

As you move through the meetings you may want to dispense with any issues that you think might take up unnecessary time in the Circle. This must be done with extreme caution, because you cannot know ahead of time what is really bothering someone. For example, you will want to remove any disputes about the facts of an event so the conversation does not get bogged down in technicalities. It may not matter if an event happened on a Tuesday or a Friday. You will want each person to tell you what happened when you meet with them, but you will also want them to focus on the important issues or the roots of the problem.

In the last few meetings, I will often begin to share factual information that is common to all participants. This is to let the participants know that these facts are not likely to be discussed in the Circle. I might say something like this:

I have heard [without disclosing any names] that Kelly dropped a box of tools on Raja's foot last month and that Raja took two days off as a result. I also heard that Raja does not eat his lunch in the lunch room any more. I also understand that there is an issue about scheduling shifts. Tell me about these situations from your perspective.

This narrowing of issues makes the Circle much more effective. Just be aware that the first meeting you have will be very different from the last meeting. For this reason, you may want to meet the first few people again and clarify with them what will likely be discussed in the Circle. I also like to meet with the key players twice.

Seek Informed Consent

Each participant must understand the process enough to be able to agree to participate. Remember that each person's attendance is voluntary. The best way to achieve informed consent is to say:

Thank you for meeting with me and sharing your perspective. I see you have been impacted by the conflict and have a unique perspective to bring to the Circle. I know you could contribute and I will likely invite you to the circle. Can you come on the date set?

It is best to put forward such an invitation rather than ask a participant directly whether they want to come. If they say no, then you will be in a bit of a bind. Let the person know how valuable it is for them to be there—for themselves, for other participants and for the group as a whole.

Acknowledge their reservations or fears and ask them what you could do to make the Circle safer for them. One approach is to ask each person who they would like to sit beside. This does two things. It helps participants begin to visualize what a Circle might look like and begin to get comfortable with it. It also demonstrates that the facilitator cares and will work hard to make the Circle safe.

Before ending each individual meeting, ask participants what they would like to have happen as a result of the Circle. They may already have several ideas or they may go away to ponder the question. The question helps participants prepare for the final stage of the Circle, when an action plan is developed. It also helps them really focus on their true needs or desires. For example, most people simply want things to be better [, which is an admirable goal but not a specific plan?]. This question also allows individuals to leave the meeting on a positive note.

The meeting is successful if each participant has confidence in the process and trusts the facilitator's ability to guide the Circle.

Select and Invite Participants

Once you have met with those you think are impacted and involved, you will need to decide whom to invite to the Circle. This decision is based on a number of factors and making the final selection can be something of an art. Here are some factors to take into consideration:

- Does this person have something critical to add to the discussion?

- Does this person have a need to share something with the group?

- Does this person have a perspective that no one else could provide?

- Does this person play a critical role in the group?

- Is this person necessary as a support person for someone else?

- Does this person want to attend simply out of curiosity?

- Is this person's presence likely to shut down the conversation?

- Does this person want to come?

If a person refuses to come, I do not force them to do so. I do, however, explain the consequences of their decision—and request their reasons. There are usually only two reasons for not wanting to come—a sense that they have nothing to contribute or fear.

If a person does not believe they have something to contribute, I ask them to explain. In some situations, a person may truly have nothing to add, or their participation may not be critical. More common, however, is that a person is simply uncomfortable about coming to the Circle. If this is so, we talk about ways to help that person feel safer. Here are some suggestions for increasing a participant's sense of comfort:

○ she can sit next to the facilitator

○ he can sit between two of his best friends or colleagues

○ she can remain silent the whole time

○ he can leave if he feels the need (with the facilitator's permission)

It's possible someone may not want to participate in the Circle under any circumstance. Because a Circle is voluntary, this situation is usually resolved in one of two ways. The individual may eventually agree to come, since not showing up would result in them being "left out." Or the individual may not attend, and this may not have a significant impact on the Circle. Here is a sample script of what to say if someone absolutely refuses to come:

Although I would like you to be at the Circle, I will be holding the Circle, even if you cannot be there. For this reason, I want to explain to you what will likely happen if you do not attend. Your absence may not impact the conversation significantly. As you know, each of the issues we have discussed in our meetings and various perspectives will be shared. Often, others will try to articulate your perspective, to make the whole situation make sense. They will not do a very good job, since they won't know what you know. The group will come to a common understanding about what happened and come up with a solution about how to repair any harm and how to move forward. You will not be there to share your thought or opinions or to make any suggestions. At the end of the day the group will come up with an action plan for your entire group. I know you do not want to come, but in my experience, those who do not attend later wish they had. They often feel that they have lost an opportunity to share their perspectives about what really happened.

This script demonstrates why it is necessary to clarify this with a person who might be hesitant about participating in the Circle.

Once you have selected those who will be invited you will need to inform each of them and confirm details of the event. This can be done by phone or in a memo confirming their attendance. In this memo it is best to list all participants so that everyone knows who will be in the Circle. Always include a contact number in case someone cannot attend.

Design a Seating Plan and Select the First Speaker

Just like choosing participants, there is a bit of an art to designing the seating plan. As a general rule it is best if people in conflict do not sit near each other. Keeping in mind that safety is your main goal, try to surround those most vulnerable with those who support them. If possible ask each person who they would like to sit next to, offering no guarantees.

You may also want to invite one person to speak first. The next chapter describes two possible conversation methods: talking stick and script. If you use a script, you will need to invite one person to begin the conversation. Here is a sample conversation you might have with one of the participants:

> *I need someone to begin the Circle conversation. During our meeting you told me about your role and perspective, and I think that what you have to say is a good starting point to the conversation. I know it is sometimes difficult to start, but I will help you articulate what you would like to say. Your comments can range from a few sentences to your whole story. How does this sound?*

Once you have invited all the participants, designed a seating plan and selected the first speaker, you will be ready to facilitate your Corporate Circle.

CHECKLIST: How to Prepare Circle Participants

Step 1. Prepare a memorandum to Circle participants to hand out at the individual meetings (see sample that follows)

Step 2. Make copies of *Corporate Circles at a Glance* (see chapter 1) to hand out at each meeting

Step 3. Meet with those impacted, following this format:

- ☐ introduce yourself and discuss confidentiality
- ☐ describe the Corporate Circle process
- ☐ answer questions about the process
- ☐ discuss participant's hopes and expectations
- ☐ describe what happens next

Step 4. During each meeting do the following:

- ☐ prepare participants for what will happen in the Circle
- ☐ help participants articulate facts, thoughts and feelings
- ☐ help participants contemplate other perspectives
- ☐ identify key events or issues for the Circle
- ☐ seek informed consent

Step 5. Select and invite participants

Step 6. Design a seating plan

Step 7. Select the first speaker

SAMPLE: Memoranda to Circle Participants

To: [Name of Participant]
From: [Name of Facilitator]
Date: [Date]
Re: The Corporate Circle Process
As you know, I will be meeting with you this week. This memorandum summarizes what I will tell you in our individual meetings:

I am a lawyer and independent conflict consultant. I have been asked to hold a group meeting called a Corporate Circle.

Before doing that, I will meet with those involved or impacted by the recent conflict or situation. This will include all immediate staff and can include others outside the workplace.

I will hold one Corporate Circle on [date] for about three to five hours. Although I decide who will be invited, I welcome your input.

During the Circle each person will share opinions and feelings about what has been happening in the workplace, how best to repair the harm and how to prevent further conflict. Each person will be given an opportunity to speak openly and candidly and is invited to explain the impact of the events at a personal and professional level.

My role is to facilitate the discussion and enable the group to consider solutions while keeping the conversation on track.

I will keep everything you tell me completely confidential, and you will be asked to keep everything we discuss here and in the Circle confidential.

A final action plan will be created by the group at the end of the Circle. It will be disclosed to others only to the extent the group wishes.

The ultimate goal of a Corporate Circle is to transform the conflict and build trusting work relations.

If you have any questions, please phone me at [phone number].

Chapter 6

How to Facilitate a Corporate Circle

Be assured that if you knew all you would pardon all.

— Thomas Kempis

If you want to make peace, you do not talk to your friends. You talk to your enemies.

— Moshe Dayan

You are lost the instant you know what the result will be.

— Juan Gris

So far you have learned how to create a Circle and how to prepare for a Circle including how to meet with participants. In this chapter you will learn how to facilitate a Circle.

At this point you may be wondering whether you are qualified or able to conduct a Circle. This really depends on a number of factors. Although the Corporate Circle process is deceptively simple, it can take enormous skill and confidence to facilitate a Circle.

Real life. Several years ago I attended a seminar for lawyers to brush up on my mediation skills. I recall the seminar leader emphasizing the need to listen and paraphrase. In her words, "teaching lawyers how to mediate a dispute required more unlearning than learning." In the role plays I recall several lawyers quickly intervening when the disputants appeared to be stuck. Only a few appeared comfortable enough to allow the parties to sit in silence or express their deeper feelings or emotions. Good mediators stand out in this regard. They not only have the ability or skill to mediate but they have a demeanor that invites people to open up. Most importantly, they have the confidence to allow the situation to take on its own natural course towards resolution, often unprompted. This is also true for Circle facilitators.

In order to conduct a Circle effectively, a facilitator should have certain knowledge, skills and attitudes. This knowledge includes the Circle process described here and a basic understanding of dispute resolution principles and practices. The skills required include conflict resolution skills such as the ability to listen, speak, paraphrase, summarize and interview. The attitudes include a demeanor of respect and a desire to empower the group to solve its own problems and create its own bonds. It includes intent of curiosity and compassion.

Related to attitude is confidence. This confidence enables a facilitator to allow a group to speak candidly with almost no intervention at all from the facilitator. This often means sitting silently for some time in the Circle.

Another requirement is neutrality. A Circle facilitator must not only be neutral but must also be perceived as neutral. This means that Circle participants must have complete confidence in the ability and integrity of the facilitator to conduct the Circle in a way in which they will be safe. In practical terms this means that an employee in an organization could only facilitate a Circle inside that organization if facilitator could ensure impartiality and complete confidentiality.

If a Corporate Circle is set up properly, it will require very little "active" facilitation. If participants are prepared and the timing is right, then conducting the Circle tends to be fairly straightforward. The main skill required of a facilitator is a type of guiding that from the outside appears almost invisible. It involves watching, listening, acknowledging, waiting, monitoring the energy and allowing the Circle to unfold naturally. This chapter discusses:

- the role of the Circle facilitator
- the evolution of a Circle conversation
- what to do before the Circle
- the four stages of a Corporate Circle
- two different methods to guide the conversation
- what to do after the Circle

The Role of the Circle Facilitator

One of the unique aspects of a Corporate Circle is the role of the facilitator. This is the person who creates and maintains the

Circle. Those who have facilitated meetings or seminars often find Corporate Circle facilitation quite different than what they are accustomed to.

It is useful to compare teachers, managers and mediators to Circle facilitators. A teacher facilitates student learning by providing instruction and directing the conversation so that specific learning is triggered. A manager facilitates team learning by seeking the input of a group and synthesizing these ideas for purposes of decision making. A mediator facilitates two or more people in conflict by helping them discuss their situation and directing them toward a solution.

In a Corporate Circle the facilitator does not instruct, control or direct. A Circle facilitator is the guardian of the Circle and is primarily responsible for safeguarding the process. Although facilitators may encourage conversation, the main role of the facilitator is to "hold open the center" of the Circle open so that a common understanding can emerge through voluntary participation and open dialogue.

It is often difficult for beginner Circle facilitators to simply trust the process and allow the thoughts, feelings and emotions of the participants to emerge in what would appear at times to be a somewhat random way. It never ceases to amaze me how an authentic conversation will unfold. Even knowing the stories and perspectives in advance could never prepare a Circle facilitator for what will emerge in the Circle.

The facilitator must be completely neutral and independent and *appear* completely neutral at all times. The facilitator must demonstrate a type of impartial awareness and presence. This comes most naturally for those who have a sense of compassion for each person in the Circle and for those who believe that the contribution of each person is valuable and necessary to moving forward. A good facilitator is alert, adaptable and honest.

There are particular actions that should be avoided in a Corporate Circle. Since the ideal demeanor is impartial awareness, the facilitator should not show any particular interest in or agreement with any particular person or topic. The facilitator should not actively mediate the conversation or alter what is being said. She should never paraphrase or suggest an outcome.

Ultimately the facilitator will assist the group in working out the details of how to move forward in the form of an action plan. Only at this stage can the facilitator summarize or synthesize ideas. It would still be improper to suggest any ideas of her own.

The Evolution of a Circle Conversation

The conversation in a Corporate Circle will be in constant movement. It will expand and contract, move fast and then slow, have highs and then lows. Just when it appears to be slowing down, it may suddenly speed up. Just when you think an individual is going to shout, peace settles on the Circle. It is intriguing to observe how humans interact. A good facilitator will recognize these shifts and know how to respond.

The conversation will evolve as it moves through stages. By understanding these stages, you will be better able to embrace the ebbs and flows of the Circle and have confidence that the dialogue will unfold naturally. The typical evolution of the conversation in a Corporate Circle involves three phases: discomfort, heightened emotions and calm collaboration.

Phase 1. Discomfort

At the start of a Circle, there is usually a feeling of slight discomfort. Participants are curious about what will happen but they are also skeptical. People tend to be nice and pleasant and generally want to be seen as cooperative. The first few comments in the Circle tend to be supportive but superficial. If the group is in serious conflict, there will be silence for some time. This is normal and should be expected.

At this stage it is important for the facilitator to be positive, confident and relaxed. The Circle process is deliberately paced to allow for comfort levels to grow somewhat naturally, in an unforced way. The first hour or so is often spent just warming up to the conversation.

> **Real life.** During one Corporate Circle the conversation continued for about an hour without anyone saying much of any significance. Several mentioned how much they liked working for the particular company and how much they liked their jobs. There was no indication that anything was wrong. I began to think that perhaps the group was not ready to have the conversation and was contemplating ways to spark a discussion. Then all of a sudden one of the quietest members of the group stood up and began speaking in a very loud voice. He said something like "I am sick and tired of all this talk

about how everything is so wonderful and how we are all working together. That is all BS and I don't want to waste any more time listening to this crap." A few people laughed and then one by one the others began to speak about what was really going on.

Phase 2. Heightened Emotions

Once people are comfortable they will be more candid about their thoughts and feelings. And as they show their deeper thoughts and feelings, differences begin to surface. This second phase involves heightened emotions and some conflict. During this phase, participants are not as polite or worried about controlling their feelings. Participants begin to have more authentic conversations and in doing so disclose opinions that are not often shared. At this stage the conversation goes deeper—though at times it appears to be on the verge of falling apart. Some people go completely silent.

Corporate Circles encourage the expression of feelings, and it is through this expression that participants are able to move from negative to positive feelings about others. This is supported by the theory of human affect developed by Silvan Tomkins and articulated by Donald Nathanson in his book *Shame and Pride* (1992). This theory describes the following nine basic human affects and how people move from negative affects to positive affects:

- dissmell

- anger-rage

- fear-terror

○ disgust

○ distress-anguish

○ shame-humiliation

○ surprise-startle

○ interest-excitement

○ enjoyment-joy

O'Connell, Wachtel and Wachtel describe how participants in a victim-offender conference move through similar emotional states:

> When participants respond to the scripted questions, they may express any or all of those negative affects or feelings. Anger, distress, fear and shame are diminished through sharing. Their expression helps to reduce their intensity. As the conference proceeds people experience a transition characterized by the neutral affect of surprise-startle. Victims, offenders and their supporters are usually surprised by what people say in the conference and how much better they begin to feel. When the conference reaches the agreement phase, participants are usually expressing the positive effects of interest-excitement and enjoyment-joy. (p. 25)

At this stage the facilitator must remain calm. For example, if someone begins to cry, the facilitator should try to withhold her emotions or at least be the last to cry. In a Corporate Circle participants may begin with a sense of fear but will eventually get to a sense of interest and enjoyment.

Phase 3. Calm Collaboration

The third and final phase involves calm collaboration. At this stage individuals move past their individual differences and develop a deep sense of connectedness. The kind of conversations that emerge are of a caliber that could never be achieved in the prior two phases.

Members treat each others as colleagues and speak with an intent that is more genuine and supportive. Scott Peck, in his book *A Different Drummer*, calls this stage *emptiness* because it consists of emptying ourselves of the beliefs and assumptions that prevent us from really hearing the other members. At this phase participants have a sense of hope for the future. Now the facilitator can play a more active role while the participants begin to think about ways to move forward and prepare an action plan.

What to do Before the Circle

The facilitator takes on their role before the Circle formally begins. The facilitator will have met with each of the participants and will be familiar with their names. He must set up the room, must greet each of the participants and must ensure they are comfortable for the whole time they are together.

The room should be set up beforehand. The circle of chairs must be as round as possible. If there are more than 30 people, two circles can be formed, one inside the other. If this is necessary, it is best to have the outside circle raised up or the inner circle lowered down. The important thing is that each of the participants can see each other person when they speak.

One useful tip is to mark each of the chairs with the names of the participants. This way each will know not only where they are sitting but also where others are sitting. If someone raises a concern about the seating plan, it is best to have a conversation with this person before everyone sits down.

The facilitator should also bring tissues and a talking piece. The talking piece can be any object that can be passed around to each speaker. Typical talking pieces include feathers, stones, sticks, rulers, or pencils. An ideal piece has meaning to that particular group.

The Four Stages of a Corporate Circle

There are four distinct stages to a Corporate Circle. Each stage is equally important and should not be rushed over or skipped. Each stage is designed to set the foundation for the next, and so on. The stages consist of the Opening, the Conversation, the Action Plan and the Closing.

Stage 1. The opening

The Opening of the Circle sets the tone for the entire Circle so must be done with care and attention. There are two parts to the opening of a Corporate Circle: calling the circle and checking in.

During the calling of the Circle, the facilitator will do the following:

- ○ invite each of the participants to sit in their designated spot

- ○ introduce him or herself

- ○ clarify the purpose and outcomes of the Circle

- ○ advise about departures and breaks

- ○ ask if there are any questions

For example, the facilitator might say something like this:

Thank you all for coming here today. As you know we will be meeting in this Corporate Circle for about three to five hours. We have come to talk about some events that have taken place over the past short while and how we can make things better. Specifically we are here to talk about the recent departure of Sally Evans and Stella Jennings, and other events. I would like you to tell me your perceptions about what happened, how it impacted you, and how you would like to move forward.

I have met with each of you and heard a bit about what has been happening. I have identified some triggering events or catalysts for conflict. My hope is that we will be able to discuss most of these events, how they have impacted you and how we can more forward.

First I will ask each of you introduce yourselves around the Circle. After that we will begin the conversation. I will focus on two questions: what has been happening in the workplace for you? and how has this impacted you? In the next stage we will talk about where to go from here and develop an action plan.

As you know, each of you are welcome to speak whenever you feel the urge. You have each promised to keep this conversation confidential. I have asked Cathy Bollings to begin the conversation.

Any questions before we begin?

It is important to speak slowly and not rush through this part. A good facilitator will scan the group and ensure that everyone looks reasonably comfortable. If not, they may want to wait a few minutes to allow people to ask questions.

After the calling of the circle there is a brief Check-In when each person introduces themselves. The participants can simply state their name and their position or, if the group is smaller, describe their hopes for the Circle. Each speaker should not be interrupted during this time, and a talking piece (explained below) can be used to support this process. Here is what the facilitator might say:

Okay, we are ready to begin.

Jim, do you want to introduce yourself, then pass the talking piece to the next person?

Some facilitators like to introduce each of the participants, while others like the participants to introduce themselves. It helps everyone to hear the voices of each person at the very beginning, but if people are feeling particularly nervous, I will introduce each person to warm up the atmosphere and show that I am there and know they are there.

If you're using the talking piece method (described below), you can simply hand the piece or other object to the person beside you. Since no one is forced to speak, that person can either speak or pass on the object until someone feels ready to speak. The piece goes around and around the Circle until the conversation is exhausted.

If you are using the script method (also described below), the facilitator should ask a person beforehand to speak first. This speeds up the process by breaking the silence that always occurs in the beginning. I usually select the person who has been most connected to the conflict and often the one who is being blamed for much of the conflict.

Stage 2. The conversation

There are two main ways to facilitate a Circle conversation. The first is to allow the conversation to move around the circle, usually by a passing around a talking piece. The other is the script method, whereby the facilitator follows a two-part script. Each method is described below. The facilitator's role is similar for both.

The role of the facilitator at the Conversation stage is primarily to observe the Circle, keep track of who speaks and keep track of time. The facilitator will watch and listen, monitor the energy level, watch the contribution of each member and intervene only when absolutely necessary. Particular care must be taken with the timing of any interventions and the manner is which they are done.

Although not all participants need to speak, the facilitator can help open up space for those who might be hesitating. For example, if I see one person leaning into the Circle but not speaking, I will simply make eye contact to let them know I see them. If the room later goes silent I will look at that person and see if they are ready to speak. This eye contact is a very powerful tool in a Corporate Circle.

The facilitator keeps track of time mostly to ensure that certain topics or participants do not take over the entire conversation. Usually the Circle will self-correct, but if it does not, the facilitator must step in.

On occasion, the facilitator may need to be more forceful in keeping the conversation on track. However, there is a real danger to intervening too strongly. The focus shifts to the facilitator and away from the participants, and the momentum of the conversation may slow significantly or even stop. When this happens it can take some time to get it moving again.

Even questions can interfere, so should be used only if the room has been quiet for some time. One useful skill is the ability to ask open-ended questions. These are questions that cannot be answered with a yes or no. They invite further elaboration. Here are some examples—all essentially requests for more information.

- ○ Please tell us more.

- ○ I am sensing that this is important. Can we speak more about it?

- ○ I wonder if someone would like to respond.

The facilitator should model good communication and should be particularly aware of their tone when speaking.

The talking piece method

The talking piece method involves each person speaking without interruption. This is a very powerful way to share, since each participant has specifically designated time and is permitted to speak about anything that comes to mind. The other members of the Circle sit quietly and listen. Here are some of the advantages of the talking piece:

The talking piece helps to manage the discussion of very emotional issues. Emotions can be expressed without the emotions taking over the dialogue. Because participants must wait for the talking piece to speak they cannot respond without thinking. Because the talking piece must go around the full circle, it prevents two individuals from getting into a back-and-forth emotional exchange. If the words of one participant anger another, multiple members of the circle may address the issues raised before the talking piece reaches the angry participant, thus relieving the angry participant from a sense of needing to defend him/herself alone. (Pranis in Engel, 2000, p. 206)

Although the facilitator may wish to impose time lines for the whole conversation, there are no limits on the amount of time designated to each speaker.

The facilitator decides when to end and will want to ensure that there has been sufficient conversation about what has been happening and how it has impacted the participants.

The script method

The other method of facilitation is the script method. The script as outlined here was designed for the victim-offender conferencing process, a process that brings together criminals, their victims, and their families. It was designed in the early 1990s in New Zealand and Canada and has been used and tested around the world.

It is based on psychological theories that show that people pass through many emotional states as they work toward understanding what they have done and its impact on others. These emotional states are necessary to transform conflict to collaboration. The script and the whole conversation are based on the following three questions:

- o What has been happening?

- o How has this impacted you?

- o Where you would like to go from here?

These three questions have their roots in basic conflict resolution technique. Marshall Rosenberg in his book *Nonviolent Communication* instructs people in conflict to break the conversation into the following parts: observations, feelings, needs and requests. Similarly, when I teach people how to resolve conflict, I tell them to break the conversation into the following three parts or three Fs: facts, feelings and future:

- ○ *Facts.* Describe the behavior that you saw using "I" statements. For example, "I saw you having lunch with my old boss yesterday." Stick to the facts and not opinions.

- ○ *Feelings.* Describe how the behavior made you feel or impacted you. Do not blame or jump to conclusions. For example, "It made me feel bad because I had confided in you my feelings about him."

- ○ *Future.* Describe what you need to prevent this event from happening again. For example, "I need to know that what I say to you stays with you."

These are the three basics steps of conflict resolution. As you will see below, the script-based conversation divides the conversation into these three parts. The first two parts take place during the Conversation stage and the third part takes place in the Action Plan stage.

Although those who facilitate victim-offender conferencing recommend that facilitators stick to a tightly worded script, I have found that this is not necessary if you have well-developed speaking, listening and facilitation skills. The most important thing is to keep the three parts as separate as possible.

In the first part of the script-method conversation the participants talk about the events or situations that have occurred in the past. This is a fairly neutral conversation since the facts are usually easy to describe, often common to all participants, usually historical and have been processed during the one-on-one meetings. Here is the script that I use:

> *As you know, we will be spending the next few hours talking about three things: what has been happening in the workplace, how that has impacted each of you, and where you would like to go from here. Now, about the facts: tell me what has been happening.*

> *Probes:*
>
> ○ And then what happened?
>
> ○ Take us through step –by –step.
>
> ○ And what were you thinking?

In the second part the conversation is about feelings. The facilitator directs the conversation to the impacts of the events. At this time the conversation begins to take a new shape. It shifts from neutral to emotional as participants describe how others' actions impacted them and how they interpreted events and situations. Although some emotions will emerge in the first part of the conversation, and they should, they now become the focus of the conversation. Here is the script that I use after a full discussion of the facts:

Now, about the impact, tell me about how these events have impacted each of you.

Probes:

○ *How did you feel when it happened?*

○ *How do you feel now?*

○ *How have things been since?*

○ *Who else might be impacted?*

Although some facilitators like to stop the conversation after the first part before moving on to the second part, I have found that the line between the first and second part is usually blurred. Participants tend to speak about what they are comfortable with. As they gain more comfort, they speak about more personal things.

As a Circle facilitator I know that the conversation is moving to the second part when people start talking in a more passionate way. This stimulates more emotions in each of the participants, and unless I really feel that the facts have not been discussed enough, I will allow the conversation to evolve naturally without telling the group that we are now moving to part 2.

Once the facts and the impacts have been thoroughly canvassed, it is best to make a clear transition or break before moving to the final part. This transition is a critical part of the process. I call this part the *Transformation and Apology*. This is the time when participants can stop and think about what has been said and finally put it behind them. Often they apologize. Here is what I typically say at this point:

> *We have heard about what has happened and how people have been affected. Before we move on, is there anything anyone would like to say to anyone else? I will dedicate the next five minutes to open sharing before moving to the next stage of the Circle.*

I introduce a silent pause to allow for any feelings of remorse to surface and dispel. This time is perhaps the most impactful time for participants. It gives participants the opportunity to finally say what they really want to say, especially to those whom they have harmed. Here are some typical comments at this stage:

- "I am sorry."
- "I never knew that you felt this way."
- "I never knew that what I did had such an impact on you."

Often participants rise from their chairs and cross the room to shake hands or hug another participant.

As stated, the key to using the script is to try to keep the three parts separate: facts, feelings and future—and ensure each is discussed thoroughly. So, for example, if someone starts talking about solutions in the Conversation stage, a facilitator might say "That sounds like a solution. Maybe we can table that until the next stage, when we discuss your action plan."

Stage 3. The action plan

The third stage of the Circle involves creating a Circle action plan. This is a completely separate part of the conversation. In this part the future is discussed. Here is the script I use at this stage:

> We will now move to the final part of the Circle. At this stage you will come up with ideas about how to repair any harm and how to move forward. Although many suggestions have emerged during our discussions, I will now take out a blank piece of paper (or flip chart) and record your ideas. This will become your Circle action plan. When all the ideas have been canvassed we can discuss how these ideas could be implemented. I will then close the Circle and ask each of you to sign the action plan. Any questions? If not I will pass the talking piece around the Circle and ask each of you to speak to the following question: What would you like to see happen as a result of our Circle today?

The conversation consists of each person simply saying what they would like to have happen after the Circle. The facilitator writes down everything exactly as it is said. When the group feels it has canvassed enough ideas, there will be a brief discussion about how to implement these ideas. Although it is not possible to discuss detailed implementation, there must be some sort of plan. Here is the script I use at this stage:

> We have a long list of ideas and solutions. Without going into a lot of detail, how could this list be implemented?

[Then I ask the following specific questions:]

○ How can we be sure the suggestions will be acted on?

○ What is the timing for each?

○ Who else needs to know about this action plan (e.g., those not in attendance or perhaps department managers)?

Often a group will decide to have another meeting to clarify the action plan, refine the list and prioritize the suggestions. Although some participants may want to begin this work right after the Circle, this is not recommended. It is better to let things settle and come to these ideas fresh on another day.

The final action plan is the written version of the ideas and the method of implementation. After the Circle conversation ends, the facilitator will write up the plan and have it signed by all participants immediately following the Circle. Copies are usually made for each of the participants to take with them.

If desired, the facilitator can later type up the action plan and send it to the group. The original usually stays with the facilitator. A sample action plan can be found at the end of this chapter.

Stage 4. The closing

The final stage involves a brief Check-Out and formal closing. In a process similar to the Check-In, participants go around the circle and make a brief comment. Unlike the Opening, participants are asked to simply provide one or two short closing remarks. The facilitator should allow a few minutes of silence before beginning the Check-Out to allow people to collect their thoughts. The participants can choose not to say anything. Each speaker should not be interrupted during this time, and a talking piece can be used.

The final closing is a powerful aspect of the Circle and should not be rushed or, worse yet, skipped. The facilitator will thank everyone for coming, remind them of the purpose of the group and the confidentiality requirement, and remind them about where they will go from here. The facilitator's main role at this stage is to mark the closing of the Circle so that the members can go back to their daily activities. Here's a sample script:

> *Thank you all for engaging in this conversation today. This has been a very productive morning. I want to thank you each personally for sharing your stories. I know it is not always easy. Remember that the goal of this Circle was not just to help you resolve conflict but to help you work better together. Your action plan is a solid step toward this becoming reality. Please remember that this conversation is confidential. I am formally closing the Circle. Best of luck.*

Although most of participants feel relieved to have had a conversation and generally feel good about airing their frustrations, many will also feel a bit remorseful. They might feel they have said things that were not appropriate and might be anxious about how others will treat them afterwards. The facilitator may wish to let participants know that these feelings may occur and that this is normal. I also make sure each person has a number to call in case they want to talk about the process afterwards. This could be my number that of an employee assistance person in or outside the company.

Ideally try to schedule some social time after the Circle to permit for an adjustment back to regular conversation. Sharing food can show a common bond.

After the Circle

Although there is no formal follow-up to a Circle, it is good practice for the facilitator to phone and check in to see how things are going. In some cases the action plan will include an evaluation component whereby the facilitator will be asked to hold another Corporate Circle in six months to have a conversation about the success of the action plan. This is highly useful for those groups who are likely to revert back to old patterns and old ways of doing things.

Format for a follow-up meeting

In many situations I am asked back to lead a follow-up meeting to discus the action plan and develop a strategy so it can be put it into action. Although not a Corporate Circle per se, the group sits in a circle and the following Circle Meeting format is used. The format follows stages similar to those of a Corporate Circle, namely the Opening, Check-In, Conversation, Check-Out and Closing. The meeting can be held at the same location and can last up to four hours.

The opening

The facilitator first asks the participants to sit in a circle. The seating arrangement does not matter. It is best for members to sit where they feel most comfortable, since this adds to a sense of safety. Once everyone is sitting down, the facilitator will call the Circle and describe the purpose of the meeting.

The check-In

After the Opening there is a brief Check-In. During the Check-In participants pass a talking piece around the Circle and briefly say how they are feeling and what they hope for during the Circle time. This usually takes two to three minutes per person. Each speaker should not be interrupted during this time. The Check-In is intended to open the conversation and also to identify issues for discussion.

The conversation

Three types of conversation can be used in a Circle Meeting. The *talking piece*, the most common method, involves a facilitator simply passing a talking piece or other object around the Circle. Individuals can speak or pass the piece on to the next person. The talking piece is passed around and around until the topic is exhausted. Each person is usually allowed to speak without interruption for about five minutes. Some Circles allocate specific time limits for the whole conversation or for each individual. Some Circles use a timer to ensure compliance. The key is to ensure that everyone has the amount of time they need, without feeling rushed.

Another method of conversation is *brainstorming*. This is useful in situations where the group is searching for creative ideas. The facilitator asks participants to call out suggestions in no particular order. All suggestions are recorded and are not judged or reflected upon. They are simply listed on a piece of paper. Once the brainstorming dwindles, the ideas put forward can be listed on a flip chart and organized, condensed or prioritized.

A final method of conversation is the *dialogue method*. In this conversation the person who is most concerned about the topic speaks first, then places a talking piece in the center of the circle. Those who wish to speak pick up the talking piece, then return it to the center when they are finished. This type of conversation trends to create more of a dialogue and tends to spiral quickly, unlike the talking piece method, which tends to produce a more paced and predictable conversation.

The aim of each of these conversations is to come up with a more detailed action plan. The facilitator will write out a plan and have each of the participants sign it at the end of the meeting.

The check-out

After the Conversation there is a brief Check-Out. In a process similar to the Check-In, participants go around the circle and briefly say how they are feeling. The Check-Out should take about two minutes per person. Each speaker should not be interrupted during this time, and a talking piece can be used.

The closing

The Closing lasts only a few minutes. After everyone has spoken around the circle, the facilitator will call the Circle to a close. This is usually done by saying something like the following:

> *I am calling this Circle to a close. Thank you for providing a space for the Circle conversation. Thank you to [name each member] for participating today.*

Ideally there should be some social time after the Circle Meeting to permit for an adjustment back to regular conversation.

Circle guidelines

If a group is really struggling, it helps to have the members agree to some meeting rules or principles before beginning the Circle Meeting. Each person agrees to these principles before getting together. Here is the list of principles I use in my Circle Meetings.

- o We will treat each other as equals.
- o We will keep conversations confidential.
- o We are committed to this group and to this process.
- o We will be open-minded.

- We will speak openly, with respect and from our own perspective.
- We will listen with curiosity and without judgment.
- We will share decision making.
- We will share leadership.

If everyone adheres to principles like these in a Circle Meeting, they increase their chances of having a richer and more meaningful conversation.

How you ultimately facilitate a Corporate Circle will depend on your unique skills, abilities and approach. Armed with an understanding of the role of facilitator, the evolution of the conversation and the four stages—and a bit of practice—you should be able to facilitate Circles for both conflict resolution and team building.

CHECKLIST: Preparing the Day Before

1. Are the participants ready?

- Have you met with all participants?
- Are participants familiar with the Circle process?
- Do participants know the time and location of the Circle?
- Do participants know who will be attending?
- Do participants have a sense of what they might say?
- Is anyone not attending? If so, have you spoken to them?

2. Is the location ready?

- ☐ Is the room open?
- ☐ Do you have a contact name for the room setup?
- ☐ Is the room set up well before the Circle?
- ☐ Is there a DO NOT DISTURB sign for the door?
- ☐ Have refreshments been arranged?

3. Are you ready?

- ☐ Do you know everyone's names and positions?
- ☐ Have you identified a number of triggering events?
- ☐ Do you know the reporting structures?
- ☐ Are you relaxed, focused, centered, and do you hold a positive intent?

4. Have you got what you need?

- ☐ Blank paper and pens
- ☐ Seating plan
- ☐ Talking piece
- ☐ Stickers for placing names on the seats
- ☐ Script and probing questions
- ☐ Several boxes of tissue
- ☐ Phone number of an employee assistance person

SAMPLE: Corporate Circle Action Plan

We held a Corporate Circle on [date] at [location] and agreed to the following:

We agree:

- ○ to create respectful environment
- ○ to create clear job descriptions
- ○ to commit to continuing this process
- ○ to commit to open and honest communication
- ○ to dedicate a meeting or more to implementing this action plan
- ○ to commit to regular meetings
- ○ to create a vision for this department
- ○ to create a values statement for this department
- ○ to review our organizational and reporting structure
- ○ to celebrate our accomplishments
- ○ to create ways to ensure continuous professional development

We will meet in one week from today for a facilitated three -hour meeting to discuss the way in which this action plan can be implemented.

This action plan will be provided to the President and the Vice-president and to Jenny Robbins (who was absent). Otherwise this action plan is confidential.

This entire action plan and its implementation plan will be revisited in six months from today at a three-hour meeting to discuss its success. We will update this action plan at that meeting.

Signed [all Circle participants' signatures]

SAMPLE: Corporate Circle Script

The following is a sample script that a facilitator can follow if using the script method of conversation in a Corporate Circle.

Welcome

Welcome everyone. Thank you all for coming today. As you know, I am [name of facilitator] and I will be facilitating this Corporate Circle.

Before we begin, I would just like to clarify a few things about the process. We will be here for about three to five hours, from 9:30 to 12:30, with extra time if need be. Lunch will be served here at 12:30, and we will take breaks at approximately one-hour intervals. If you need to go to the bathroom, just signal me. If anyone gets called away, we will take a break.

It is important that each of you gets an opportunity to speak if you wish. I will encourage you to participate and will intervene only if necessary. The only requirement is that we all stay for the entire time. Everything said in this Circle will remain confidential.

Stage 1. The opening

Calling the circle

I know that each of you wants to make things better and to create a more supportive and collaborative workplace.

This has been a difficult time for everyone, so it is important that we deal with it together. As you know, we will be spending the next few hours talking about three things:

- *what has been happening in the workplace*
- *how that has impacted each of you, and*
- *where you would like to go from here.*

Each of you is welcome speak whenever you feel the urge.

Check-In

To start, I will ask each of you introduce yourselves around the circle. After that we will begin the conversation. I have asked Cathy Bollings to begin the conversation. Any questions before we begin?

Stage 2. The conversation

Facts

Tell me what has been happening for you in the workplace. Cathy, do you want to begin?

Probes:

- *And then what happened?*
- *Take us through step by step.*
- *And what were you thinking?*

Feelings

Now, about the impact, tell me about how these events have impacted each of you.

Probes:

- *How did you feel when it happened?*
- *How do you feel now?*
- *How have things been since?*
- *Who else might be impacted?*

Transition

We have heard about what has happened and how people have been affected. Before we move on, is there anything anyone would like to say to anyone else? I will dedicate the next five minutes to open sharing before moving to the next stage of the Circle.

Stage 3. The action plan

Ideas

As you know, we have found out what has happened and how you have been affected. Now we will move to the action plan part of the Circle. At this stage we come up with ideas about how to repair any harm and to move forward. Many suggestions have emerged during our discussions. For example, [fill in details here]. I will record your ideas on a flip chart. This will become your Circle action plan. When all the ideas have been canvassed, we can discuss how these ideas could be implemented. I will then close the Circle and ask each of you to sign the action plan. Here is my question: What would you like to see happen as a result of our Circle today? [Either go around the circle or have an open conversation.]

Implementation

We have along list of ideas and solutions. Without going into a lot of detail, how could this list be implemented?

- o How can we be sure the suggestions will be acted on?
- o What is the timing for each?
- o Who else needs to know about this action plan (e.g., those not in attendance or perhaps departmental managers)?

Stage 4. The closing

Check-Out

To end this Circle I will pass the talking piece around one last time. If you would like to share how you feel right now, please do so. First I will give you a moment to collect your thoughts. [Wait a moment before passing the piece to allow participants time to gather their thoughts.]

Closing

Thank you all for engaging in this conversation today. This has been a very productive morning. I want to thank you each personally for sharing your stories. I know it is not always easy. Remember that the goal of this Circle was to not just help you resolve conflict but to help you work better together. Your action plan is a solid step toward this becoming reality. Over the next few days you may feel a bit remorseful; this is normal. Please remember that this conversation is confidential.

I am formally closing the Circle. Best of luck. I invite each of you to sign this action plan you have agreed to and then join your colleagues for lunch.

Chapter 7

The Future of Circles

Circles provide the space in which we reveal ourselves, uncover our core humanity, and allow others to feel, know, and touch us. We can't walk through the sacred space of Circles and emerge as we were. We're deepened, and from those depths, we find the power to create our worlds anew–together.
                    — Pranis, Stuart and Wedge, Peacemaking Circles

I believe that Circles will revolutionize the way we do things – in corporations, in communities, in families and in the world.

My hope is that Corporate Circles will eventually be used by all corporations around the world, not just to resolve conflict and build strong teams but to introduce a new way of being together. As Circles become part of the mainstream corporate cultures will begin to shift. People will no longer avoid confrontation and will have the confidence and skills to say what they really mean.

Candid conversations will abound. Hierarchies and cultures of mistrust will begin to fade and gossip will be replaced with kind words. Differences will welcome and all opinions will be encouraged. As a result I believe that individual and corporate creativity and effectiveness will increase.

The more we speak in Circles the more we can hear and be heard, which is the foundation of all communication. We will begin to understand better how, as humans we all share the same fundamental needs and how we are all connected in some way. Because the principles of Circles deeply humane, by using the Circle process I believe that people will begin to treat each other better. People will develop empathy and become more tolerant and accepting of others.

Although the circle process seems new to many it has ancient roots. Because of its almost natural simplicity Circles and its effectiveness the circle process can't help but find a place in the corporate world and elsewhere. As described by author Christina Baldwin in *Calling the Circle*,

> Readiness for circles is rising in the culture like yeast. Just when I think the circle is never going to work.... we get an opportunity to introduce it in places where I never expected to find receptivity. All my assumptions about where the circle will find its home are constantly being blown away. (p. 87)

I follow in Christina Baldwin's steps and borrow her words when I say that I "intend to help instill the skills of circle in a thousand ways and places." I encourage each of you to do the same.

References

Baldwin, Christina. *Calling the Circle: The First and Future Culture*. New York: Bantam Doubleday Dell, 1998.

Bohm, David. *On Dialogue*. Edited by Lee Nichol. New York, NY: Routledge, 1996.

Coloroso, Barbara. *The Bully, the Bullied and the Bystander*. New York: Harper Collins, 2002.

Coombs, Ann. *The Living Workplace*. New York: Harper Collins, 2001.

Engel, Beverly. *Women Circling the World: A Guide to Fostering Community, Healing and Empowerment*. Deerfield Beach, Florida: Health Communications, 2000.

Fitzgerald, Maureen. *A Woman's Circle. Create a peer mentoring group for advice, networking, support and connection*. CenterPoint Media, 2015.

Garfield, Charles, Cindy Spring, & Sedonia Cahill. *Wisdom Circles: A Guide to Self-Discovery and Community Building in Small Groups*. New York: Hyperion, 1998.

Gergen, David. Eyewitness to Power: The Essence of Leadership Nixon the Clinton New York: Touchstone, 2000.

Isaacs, William. *Dialogue: Dialogue and the Art of Thinking Together: A Pioneering Approach to Communicating in Business and in Life*. New York: Doubleday Currency, 1999.

Moore, David, & John McDonald. *Transforming Conflict*. New

South Wales, Australia: TJA, 2000.

Nathanson, Donald. *Shame and Pride: Affect, Sex and the Birth of the Self.* New York: W.W. Norton & Co., 1992.

O'Connell, Terry, Ben Wachtel, & Ted Wachtel. *Conferencing Handbook: New Real Justice Training Manual.* Pipersville, PA: Pipers Press, 1999.

Peck, M. Scott. *The Different Drum: Community-Making and Peace.* New York: Touchstone, 1987.

Pranis, Kay, Barry Stuart & Mark Wedge. *Peacemaking Circles: From Crime to Community.* St. Paul, MN: Living Justice Press, 2003.

Rosenberg, Marshall B. *Nonviolent Communication: A Language of Compassion.* Encinitas, CA: PuddleDancer Press, 1999.

Stone, Douglas, Bruce Patton, & Sheila Heen. *Difficult Conversations: How to Discuss What Matters Most.* New York: Viking Penguin, 1999.

Wheatley, Margaret J. *Turning to One Another: Simple Conversations to Restore Hope to the Future.* San Francisco, CA: Berrett-Koehler, 2002.

Zehr, Howard. *Changing Lenses: A New Focus for Crime and Justice.* Scottdale, PA: Herald Press, 1990.

---. *The Little book of Restorative Justice.* Intercourse, PA: Good Books, 2002.

Zimmerman, Jack, in collaboration with Virginia Coyle. *The Way of the Council.* Los Vegas, NV: Bramble Books, 1996.

About the Author

Maureen F. Fitzgerald, PhD, LLB, LLM, BComm is the founder of *Centerpoint Media*. She is a thought leader and change agent, practiced law for over 20 years and is the author of over ten books and many articles. Her mission is to use her writing to open minds and hearts – to make the world a better place.

Maureen learned about restorative justice while mediating workplace disputes and investigating sexual harassment and bullying complaints. She grew frustrated with the adversarial model and grievance process and decided to focus instead on repairing and healing relationships.

In her former life, Maureen was a labor lawyer and professor of law at two universities. Maureen has a business degree, two law degrees, a masters' degree in law from the London School of Economics and a doctorate degree in philosophy.

Always a leader of both people and ideas, Maureen speaks often about social justice, equality and open-mindedness. Her motto is: Sharing the right ideas at the right time can change the world. You can find her at www.MaureenFitzgerald.com.

Generic Use and Intellectual Property

The use of circles is growing in many ways and forms and all uses of circling are always encouraged. Maureen Fitzgerald coined the word "Corporate Circles" to reflect the process and principles described in this book, which emerged from a combination of years of learning and personal experiences. It is a specific contribution to the growing body of knowledge.

Feel free to use any parts of this book. I hope that others will build on this model and that Circles will sprout up in many different forms in many different locations.

When using the words "Corporate Circles" or the concepts in this book please acknowledge the author, and the title of this book.

Thank you.

Also by the author

Lean Out - *Shatter the glass ceiling to success, happiness and work-life balance.*

Motherhood is Madness - *Break the chains to happiness as a mother and wife.*

Occupy Women- *A manifesto for success, happiness and freedom in world run by men.*

Mindfulness Made Easy - *50 simple practices to reduce stress, create calm and live in the moment - at home, work and school.*

Wake up Sleeping Beauty - *Protect your daughter from sexism, stereotypes and sexualisation.*

Mean Girls Aren't Mean - *Stand up to cliques, bullies, peer pressure and popularity and empower girls in a radical new way.*

Gritty is the New Pretty - *Raise confident, courageous and resilient girls in a man's world.*

A Woman's Circle - *Create a peer mentoring group for advice, networking, support and connection.*

Hiring, Managing and Keeping the Best - *The complete canadian guide for employers, (with Monica Beauregard.)*

So You Think You Need a Lawyer - *How to screen, hire, manage or fire a lawyer.*